Twayne's United States Authors Series

EDITOR OF THIS VOLUME

David J. Nordloh

Indiana University

Charles W. Chesnutt

TUSAS 373

Charles W. Chesnutt

CHARLES W. CHESNUTT

By Sylvia Lyons Render

Library of Congress

TWAYNE PUBLISHERS
A DIVISION OF G. K. HALL & CO., BOSTON

Copyright © 1980 by G. K. Hall & Co.

Published in 1980 by Twayne Publishers
A Division of G. K. Hall & Co.
All Rights Reserved

Printed on permanent / durable acid-free paper and bound
in the United States of America

Library of Congress Cataloging in Publication Data

Render, Sylvia Lyons.
  Charles W. Chesnutt.

  (Twayne's United States authors series ; TUSAS 373)
  Bibliography: p. 174–81
  Includes index.
  1. Chesnutt, Charles Waddell, 1858–1932—Criticism and in-
terpretation.
PS1292.C6Z85   813'.4   80–24234
ISBN 0–8057–7272–3

Contents

About the Author

Sylvia Lyons Render received an M.A. degree from Ohio State University. She began teaching at Florida Agricultural and Mechanical University, then matriculated at the University of Wisconsin, Madison, and at George Peabody College for Teachers, Nashville. Ms. Render wrote the first dissertation on Charles Waddell Chesnutt and earned a Ph.D. degree in English.

Dr. Render accepted a professorship at North Carolina Central University in Durham, which she held until appointed to the position of Specialist in Afro-American History and Culture in the Manuscript Division of the Library of Congress. Besides participating in a number of professional organizations, she continues to lecture on college campuses and to serve as a consultant for universities, publishers, philanthropic foundations, and government agencies.

Dr. Render has received many honors, awards, and fellowships from groups such as the American Philosophical Society, the North Carolina Central Faculty Research Committee, the Duke University–University of North Carolina Cooperative Program in the Humanities, the Ford Foundation, and the National Endowment for the Humanities.

Among her publications are an edited collection, *The Short Fiction of Charles W. Chesnutt*; "Charles W. Chesnutt," *Encyclopaedia Britannica*; the introduction in Chesnutt's *The Marrow of Tradition* republished by Arno Press and *New York Times*; "The Black Presence in the Library of Congress," *Library Lectures*, ed., Caroline Wire; and articles in scholarly journals.

Preface

Race has had a telling influence on American literature. Because of it, our national culture has a piquant variety less evident in the works of a nation whose people claim a common ancestry or fewer ethnic origins. And for the first time in our national history, sustained attempts are now being made to determine the full extent of the black man's role, as creator and as character, in the development of the literature of the United States. Of greater social significance is the concerted effort of scholars and publishers to introduce to the general public obscure though competent Afro-American writers of the past.

Charles Waddell Chesnutt is one such author. The quality of his prose writings, especially the short stories and novels published between 1885 and 1905, won for him—paradoxically—only passing popularity but lasting critical praise. Chesnutt is recognized as the first Negro novelist of merit; moreover, in his treatment of theme and character, he anticipated many twentieth-century American novelists, including Richard Wright. Chesnutt is also known as the pioneer of the color line because of his realistic probing of relations not only within the Afro-American and Euro-American groups but also between them at a time when many aspects of such interaction were conveniently ignored and public discussion of them taboo. His views on many other vital issues of the day were nearer to the public sentiment of the 1980s than to the general consensus of his own time. Consequently his more serious works had only limited circulation among the predominantly well-to-do white female reading public of the late nineteenth and early twentieth centuries.[1]

Yet the original critical assessment of Chesnutt as an important writer by George Washington Cable, William Dean Howells, Walter Hines Page, and other literati has been sustained. Chesnutt is now firmly established as a minor writer in the American literary hierarchy. He is also the most important forerunner of twentieth-century black literature and was the best Afro-American writer of prose fiction until the late 1930s.

Despite his significant contribution to American letters, Chesnutt is hardly known to present-day readers, many of whom would find his views compatible with their own. Further, he, like most black writers, is still frequently overlooked or misinterpreted in general surveys, genre collections, and specialized critiques dealing with white writers of his literary stature.

In this study I shall trace Chesnutt's development as a writer, suggesting the great influence of his life and times upon the purposes, nature, and scope of his published prose. I shall show how the course of his writing follows the mainstream of American history and literature as well as the ethnic tributary of Afro-American acts and words. I shall also indicate the probable influences on Chesnutt as a writer, the kinds of writing Chesnutt produced, the major milieus of his works, the variety of his characters and the situations in which they interacted, the themes of the fiction in relation to past or contemporary issues, and style of the writings, public and critical reaction to them, and Chesnutt's legacy to literature.

I hope this work will further stimulate the interest already manifested in Chesnutt. He told his world how it appeared through his colored glasses; his work deserves now to be viewed through the clearer lenses of retrospective appraisal.

SYLVIA LYONS RENDER

Alexandria, Virginia

Acknowledgments

I cannot express the extent of my appreciation to the many individuals, institutions, and organizations that contributed in some way to the writing of this book. Nevertheless, I am pleased to have this opportunity to acknowledge my indebtedness to some of them.

For guidance and support in writing the dissertation which was the genesis of this work, Prof. Warren I. Titus of George Peabody College for Teachers. For private papers, records, and reminiscenses: Chesnutt relatives and friends, including Miss Helen M. Chesnutt, Miss Sara Chesnutt, Mrs. Ann Chesnutt Waddell, John C. Slade, Mrs. Fannie Headen, Mrs. E. T. Page, Mrs. Irene Cherry, Mrs. Armen G. Evans, William S. Braithwaite, Dr. Lyon N. Richardson, Russell H. Davis. J. D. Nobel, and Carr Liggett. For invaluable help in locating and making available research materials: Fisk University Library Staff, especially Arna Bontemps, George Gardiner, Dr. Jessie Smith, and Mrs. Ann Allen Shockley; Miss Anna Loe Russell of the George Peabody College for Teachers Library; Dr. Kermit J. Pike, Mrs. Virginia R. Hawley and Mrs. Olivia J. Martin of the Western Reserve Historical Society Library; Miss Margaret Terwilliger of the Cleveland Public Library; Mrs. Marie Baker of the Rowfant Club, Cleveland, Ohio; reference staff of the New York Public Library system, especially Mrs. Jean Blackwell Hutson and Miss Ruth Ann Stewart of the Schomburg Center for Research in Black Culture; Mrs. Dorothy Porter Wesley and James P. Johnson of the Moorland-Spingarn Research Center of Howard University; Mrs. Gloria Prescott, Mrs. Sadie G. Hughley, Mrs. Jocelyn Stevens and other members of the North Carolina Central University Library staff; Professors Arlin Turner and Clarence Gohdes, and Misses Florence E. Blakely and Mary W. Canada of Duke University; Fayetteville State University administrators, including President Charles A. Lyons and Librarian Nathalene R. Smith; Mrs. Portia Washington Pittman; Dr. Charles W. Foster; Charles L. Blockson; Mrs. Tommie W. Hoggett; Houghton Mifflin Company officials; the College Language Association; and my colleagues at the Library of Congress, especially the staff of the Manuscript Division.

For the tedious tasks which were unavoidable in the preparation and revision of the manuscript: Mrs. Julia W. Harris, Mrs. Jacob Kaplan, Mrs. Sonia Stockard, Miss Audrey Dupuy, Mrs. Carroll M. Shurney, and Profs. Ralph W. Hyde and David J. Nordloh. And, finally, for the grants which provided me with much-needed time and materials to complete this volume: the American Philosophical Society, the North Carolina Central University Faculty Research Committee, the Cooperative Program in the Humanities conducted jointly by Duke University and the University of North Carolina at Chapel Hill, the Ford Foundation, and the National Endowment for the Humanities.

Chronology

1893　Declines to buy stock in Tourgée journal.

1896　Visits Europe.

1897　Meets Walter Hines Page and other Houghton Mifflin staff.

1898　"The Wife of His Youth" in *Atlantic Monthly.*

1899　*The Conjure Woman,* collection of Uncle Julius tales, and *The Wife of His Youth and Other Stories of the Color Line* published by Houghton Mifflin. *Frederick Douglass* published by Small, Maynard. Lectures and reads his stories to groups. September 30: gives up business and sets up literary office at home.

1900　Meets William Dean Howells and other literary figures. *The House Behind the Cedars* published by Houghton Mifflin. Series of controversial essays on race issue in the *Boston Evening Transcript.*

1901　Makes southern lecture tour and publishes several articles about his observations. Begins exchange of letters with Booker T. Washington on vital issues. Instrumental in having W. H. Thomas's *The American Negro* withdrawn from circulation. *The Marrow of Tradition* published by Houghton Mifflin. Chairs the Committee on Colored Troops for the 35th National Encampment of the Grand Army of the Republic in Cleveland in September. Reopens and expands stenographic services firm.

1903　Contributes "The Disfranchisement of the Negro" to *The Negro Problem: A Series of Articles by Representative American Negroes of Today.*

1904　Accepts membership on Committee of Twelve, organized by Booker T. Washington.

1905　*The Colonel's Dream* published by Doubleday, Page. Guest at Mark Twain's seventieth birthday party. Retires from writing as a profession. Serves as a consultant on the Negro problem. Becomes member of the Cleveland Council of Sociology.

1910　Addresses National Negro Committee (which became the National Association for the Advancement of Colored People) and later serves as member of the General Committee of the NAACP. Hospitalized with a stroke. Accepts invitation to become member of the exclusive Rowfant Club of Cleveland.

1912   Becomes member of Cleveland Chamber of Commerce. Tours Europe with daughter Helen. Visits the Samuel Coleridge-Taylors.

1913   Awarded LL.D. degree by Wilberforce University. Chairs a committee for local Perry Centenary Celebration.

1914   Helps establish Playhouse Settlement, now called Karamu House.

1915   Successfully protests showing of *The Birth of a Nation* in Ohio and, in 1917, in Cleveland.

1916   Participates in First Amenia Conference, called by Joel Spingarn.

1917   Joins National Arts Club. Protests treatment of Negro soldiers.

1920   Stricken with appendicitis and peritonitis.

1927   New edition of *The Conjure Woman* published by Houghton Mifflin.

1928   Appears before a Senate Committee in Washington to testify against the Shipstead Anti-Injunction Bill. Awarded the Spingarn Medal by the National Association for the Advancement of Colored People.

1930   "The Negro in Cleveland" in the *Clevelander* in November.

1931   "Post-Bellum—Pre-Harlem" in Part 5 of *The Colophon* in February.

1932   Dies at home, November 15.

CHAPTER 1

South-North Round Trip

When a young man starts out in life with a purpose and works *for* that purpose, he is more than apt to accomplish it.[1]

CHARLES Waddell Chesnutt was a child of change, change caused largely by caste. Since "the artist is no freer than the society in which he lives," Chesnutt's literary works reflect the impact of caste experiences upon his thought and imagination.

I *Flight*

His parents-to-be, Ann Maria Sampson, "a beautiful and spirited girl with a brilliant mind," and ambitious Andrew Jackson Chesnutt, met in 1856 under romantic circumstances. Both were members of a northbound wagon train of free colored people from the Fayetteville, North Carolina, area seeking relief from racial hostility which had been increasing since the 1830s. The "Free People of Color," with varying degrees of Negro, white, and Indian ancestry (55 percent were mulattoes, according to David Dodge), had felt few constrictions of race in the comparatively liberal atmosphere of the eighteenth century.[2] John S. Leary, a Negro lawyer and legislator of North Carolina, had stated that " 'at the time of the Declaration of Independence, there was a larger number of free Negroes in the colonial dependency . . . now comprising the State of North Carolina than [in] any other Southern State.' "[3]

When the North Carolina State Constitution was adopted in 1776, no free resident was discriminated against on the basis of race. The resulting atmosphere of freedom contributed to the increase of the population of free Negroes in North Carolina from about 5,000 (this number is supposed to include all free non-whites, but obviously excludes Indians) in 1790 to 30,463 in 1860, an increase proportionately greater than that of either the white or the slave population in the state until 1850, and in numbers exceeded only by concentrations of free Negroes in Maryland and Virginia in the South.[4] Rural rather than urban, they lived on social and economic levels ranging from upper-middle-class security down to a precarious existence scorned even by the slaves.[5]

. Chloe Sampson (the mother of Ann Maria), Ann Maria, and young Andrew Jackson Chesnutt were three of the many "best colored people" who left North Carolina because of increasingly intolerable conditions.[6] The mild economic depression of that decade and the corrosive fears of slave insurrections caused whites to institute a Free Negro Code which, after 1835, deprived free Negroes of all meaningful rights as citizens.[7] Consequently, free Negroes, who had comprised a unique patriotic segment of the North Carolina population since colonial times, were by the 1850s the hapless victims of a caste system.[8] Many of them, like the Sampsons and Chesnutts, were, as Charles W. Chesnutt later described himself in a letter to Emmett J. Scott, "so thoroughly mingled along the edges that at times it is not exactly easy to characterize an individual as belonging to one race or another."[9] After the Civil War many Negroes who had never been enslaved continued to draw a line between "those born free and those shot free" as well as to make distinctions based upon color. These mixed-bloods comprise the particular segment of the "caste within a caste" that Charles W. Chesnutt introduced into literature nearly half a century later.

During the perilous period just before the Civil War, however, larger matters of freedom and safety concerned some of the free colored people in North Carolina. In 1856 Chloe Sampson breathed a sigh of relief at getting her daughter out of Fayetteville without incident. Dynamic Ann Maria had chafed at the demeaning restrictions imposed upon her people, especially that one forbidding the teaching of slaves. A born educator, she had repeatedly risked fine, imprisonment, or from twenty to thirty-nine lashes on her bare back in order to instruct slave children secretly.[10] As the wagons wound their arduous way through Virginia and Pennsylvania, Ann Maria directed her energies to charming, cajoling, and even scolding the discouraged and the dissident. Andrew, observing, was smitten; Ann Maria was attracted. Weeks later, when he waved good-bye to the Cleveland-bound caravan to go farther west to Indiana, where he had an uncle established in business, he left his heart with Ann Maria. Therefore, although Andrew (or "Jack," as he was called by intimates) found future prospects very bright with his Hoosier kin, it was not surprising that he journeyed to Cleveland within the year. On July 27, 1857, Andrew Jackson Chesnutt and Ann Maria Sampson were married.

The newlyweds shared with Chloe Sampson the little house she had bought in a modest German neighborhood on Hudson Street. While Andrew drove a horse-powered city tramcar, Ann Maria planned how she would give their children security and happiness in those pleasant surroundings. She was especially determined that her first—and favorite—child, Charles Waddell, born June 20, 1858, would realize all her thwarted hopes by standing upright and filling a man's place in the world—that he would become "a scholar and a gentleman." During his early years, according to his daughter Helen, the young mother "endeavored to fill his heart with fine ideals and lofty principles, to imbue his mind with the spirit of courage and high endeavor. She tried to make him feel that loyalty and duty were sacred obligations."[11]

Believing that living near Oberlin College, which had no color bar, would be conducive to these ends, Ann Maria implemented her family's move to Oberlin, Ohio, that summer. However, they lived there only long enough for son Lewis to be born early in 1860. Then they returned to Cleveland, where Mother Chloe helped with the two babies and Andrew was reemployed by the city. Before serving with the Union forces as a teamster at the outbreak of the Civil War, he fathered two more boys and one girl; only his namesake, Andrew, lived past infancy.

II   *Return*

Meanwhile life went on serenely in the Sampson household and Charles entered public school before the Chesnutts moved again. Finding himself near Fayetteville, North Carolina, at the end of the war, Andrew went home. His decision to settle there was influenced both by his father's failing health and by the latter's subsequent backing of Andrew as an independent grocer.[12] When Ann Maria found out about her husband's plans, she demurred, and then rebelled. How could they give up the advantages which life in the North would afford the children? Finally she decided, dutifully, to join her husband, sustained by a tenuous hope that conditions for colored people in the South would have improved considerably since the North had been victorious in the recent conflict. Some of that hope died with the assassination of President Lincoln in 1865.

When Mrs. Chesnutt and her three little boys arrived in Fayetteville in 1866, many changes envisioned by Abraham Lincoln were already taking place. Later, under the auspices of the Freedmen's Bureau, the Howard School (which evolved into Fayetteville State University), named for Gen. O. O. Howard, Director of the Bureau, was built on land purchased by Mr. Chesnutt and other public-spirited blacks. There the Chesnutt children came under the beneficent influence of Principal Robert Harris, who devoted his life to the education of Afro-American youth.

After school Charles helped in his father's downtown grocery store. Mr. Chesnutt had become a county commissioner and justice of the peace for Cumberland County; his store was a natural gathering place for customers and hangers-on who discussed everything from currency to conjuration. The boy, busy but attentive, did not then realize that he was absorbing subject matter for some of his best stories.

At home Charles tried to share both the news and the household chores with his mother, whom he idolized. Her health failed after she bore three more babies in quick succession. Not even the helpful presence of her mother could arrest Mrs. Chesnutt's fatal decline. Thus at thirteen Charles found himself bereft of his only source of inspiration in the family circle and bound by a deathbed promise to look after five younger brothers and sisters.

Within the year Chesnutt's grocery business failed because of his too generous credit practices. He then moved the family to his farm two miles down the Wilmington Road. Soon thereafter Grandmother Chloe persuaded an eighteen-year-old cousin, Mary Ochiltree, to replace her as housekeeper and attend Howard School. "Before very long" widower Chesnutt wed Mary. They eventually had six children of their own.

III   *Growing Up*

Shortly after the move to the country, Andrew J. Chesnutt told Charles he would have to stop school and help support the family.

The youth was evidently an excellent student, for when he explained his predicament to Robert Harris, the principal immediately made him a salaried pupil-teacher. Thereafter Charles spent more time teaching than being taught; there is no evidence that he either finished Howard School or attended any other.

In addition to the "race problem," which plagued Charles W. Chesnutt in one way or another for the rest of his life, the boy suffered all the growing pains of adolescence, aggravated by loneliness during those summers when his need to work required that he reside temporarily in the small Carolina communities whose Negro school districts could afford a teacher. His conscience smote him for not sending more money home. He was dismayed by the ignorance, superstition, and narrow-mindedness of the adults who did not know "enough words for a fellow to carry on a conversation with them."[13] Thus Charles began to keep the journals which reveal him as a sensitive, ambitious personality and provide proof that he drew heavily upon his experiences and observations for many of his later writings.

In the "Aerial Architecture" (his fanciful term for daydreams) he built then and subsequently, Charles saw himself successful in many professions, including teaching, writing, and law.[14]

He became a teacher by chance and a writer by choice. His success in both professions was due largely to his lifelong passion for books and reading. Upon accepting the Spingarn Medal in 1928 he reminisced: "I was always an omnivorous reader. Indeed I cannot remember when I did not read. My maternal grandmother once remarked in my hearing that had she not been present at my delivery she could have believed that I was born with a book in my hand."[15]

Charles found few books at home to satisfy his seemingly insatiable appetite. Fortunately two prominent white citizens of Fayetteville, recognizing the boy's native ability and good breeding, gave him access to their shelves. Dr. Edward J. Lilly let Charles enjoy what was considered the finest collection in the community—most of it imported from England and Scotland—and George Haigh permitted the precocious youngster to browse at will in his well-stocked bookstore. Long before Charles reached adolescence he spent most of his spare time reading and "every cent he could call his own . . . in buying secondhand books." Out of the first paycheck over which he had complete control he bought a copy of Dickens's *Barnaby Rudge.*[16]

Whether in the comparative isolation of the country or with family and friends in Fayetteville, Chesnutt followed a schedule which showed reading as his main pastime. While teaching in the country in 1875 he noted in his journal: "I rise at 6, read till breakfast . . . [then] read till school time, one-half past 8, go to school, let out about 3 o'clock, come home and read till dusk. Then I can sit and sing, and recite pieces I have learned, and think over what I have read."[17]

In 1875 Chesnutt began teaching in Charlotte under Cicero Harris, brother of Robert Harris, and succeeded him as principal of a public school before returning to the newly established State Colored Normal School in Fayetteville in 1877 as first assistant to Principal Robert Harris and as "teacher of reading, writing, spelling, composition, and related subjects." This first state-supported teacher-training institution for the Negro population was housed on the second floor of the Howard School, still supervised by Professor Harris. Its enrollment in 1878–79 was ninety-three.

Chesnutt was the moving spirit of the Normal Literary Society. By his own example and through lectures, he tried "to inspire the young men [students] with . . . honorable ambition, an earnest desire for usefulness."[18] On many occasions Chesnutt shared with the students his belief that the American Dream could come true for any enterprising citizen. He held that prejudice against blacks in the United States was due more to their condition than to their color. Therefore respect and recognition would follow improvement of their common lot until each would be "considered . . . as a friend and brother."[19] He also felt "that many of the Southern States could well take example from North Carolina in her attitude toward the colored people."[20]

IV *Adulthood*

Chesnutt's return to Fayetteville also brought about a great change in his personal life. Vivacious Susan U. Perry, whose family was also of free colored ancestry, had begun teaching at Howard School. Encouraged by Susan, Charles declared his intentions; her parents approved of the courtship. On June 6, 1878, the couple married and set up housekeeping in her parents' home. Not until Chesnutt became principal of the Normal School in 1880 did he, his wife, and their baby girl, Ethel, move into a separate dwelling.

Between 1879 and 1883 Chesnutt pursued a variety of activities. He continued to read widely, took piano and organ lessons, and supplemented his study of foreign languages with private tutors. At the same time he was teacher and principal of the Normal School and "recapitulator" of the Literary Society; he gave private lessons in piano, organ, voice, and Latin. He also served as organist, choirmaster, and Sunday School superintendent of the historic Metropolitan African Methodist Episcopal Zion Church.

Chesnutt kept up his reading through the years. His favorite subjects, great men and good books, reflect a basic belief "that, except the living example of a pure life, there is no agency so potent for leading the youthful mind to high aspirations as good books." His high regard for the didactic end of literature became apparent in his first published story, which appeared serially in a local Negro weekly in 1872. "Its motive was the baleful effects on the youthful mind of reading dime novels."[21]

V   *Decision-Making*

Good books also had great aesthetic appeal for Chesnutt. His special delight in reading made writing his first choice as vocation or avocation. *Barnaby Rudge* moved him at seventeen to "wish I could write like Dickens, but alas I can't."[22] Again, after reading Thackeray's *Vanity Fair*, he wrote, "Every time I read a good novel, I want to write one. It is the dream of my life—to be an author!"[23] The popularity of Albion W. Tourgée's *A Fool's Errand* reinforced his desire with determination:

. . . If Judge Tourgée, with his necessarily limited intercourse with colored people and with his limited stay in the South, can write such interesting descriptions, such vivid pictures of Southern life and character as to make himself rich and famous, why could not a colored man, who has lived among colored people all his life; who is familiar with their habits, their ruling passions, their prejudices, their whole moral and social condition . . . and who, besides, had possessed such opportunities for observation and conversation with the better class of white men in the South, as to understand their modes of thinking; who was familiar with the political history of the country, and especially with all phases of the slavery question;—why could not such a man, *if he possessed the same ability*, write a far better book about the South than Judge Tourgée or Mrs. Stowe has written?[24]

With this, Chesnutt's "principal object" in keeping a journal changed from improving himself "in the art of composition" to recording "my impressions of men and things, and such incidents or conversations which take place within my knowledge, with a view to future use in literary work."[25]

A few months later the young teacher's creative imagination clamored for fuller expression:

I think I must write a book. I am almost afraid to undertake a book so early and with so little experience in composition. But it has been my cherished dream, and I feel an influence that I cannot resist calling me to the task. Besides, I do not know but I am as well prepared as some other successful writers. A fair knowledge of the classics, a speaking acquaintance with the modern languages, an intimate friendship with literature, etc., seven years experience in the school room, two years of married life, and a habit of studying character have, I think, left me not entirely unprepared to write even a book. Fifteen years of life in the South, in one of the most eventful eras of its history; among a people whose life is rich in the elements of romance; under conditions calculated to stir one's soul to the very depths;—I think there is here a fund of experience, a supply of material, which a skillful person could work up with tremendous effect.[26]

Apparently a combination of deprivation, distraction, and the demands of duty had been unable to stifle this deep-seated desire. For Chesnutt, writing was an especially satisfying means of fulfillment, and, emanating from his inmost being, would doubtless have manifested itself under any circumstances. But as he continued to articulate his thoughts and feelings, he reflected "the tensions and cross-purposes" of his southern surroundings in his "high and holy purpose for writing," which

would not be so much the elevation of the Colored people as the elevation of the Whites—for I consider the unjust spirit of caste which is so insidious as to pervade a whole nation, and so powerful as to subject a whole race and all connected with it to scorn and social ostracism . . . a barrier to the moral progress of the American people. And I would be one of the first to head a determined, organized crusade against it. Not a fierce determined onslaught; not an appeal to force, for this is something that force can but slightly affect; but a moral revolution which must be brought about in a different manner.

The Negro's part is to prepare himself for social recognition and equality; and it is the province of literature to open the way for him to get it—to accustom the public mind to the idea; and while amusing them to lead them on to the desired state of feeling.[27]

The rapid deterioration of race relations in the South after the Compromise of 1877 intensified Chesnutt's desire to put his literary theories into practice.[28] He had great hopes that the stories he could write would replace animosity and contempt with amity and concern. But his anxiety about the future of his family outweighed all other considerations. Recalling his own life in the South, he vowed silently not to expose his children to the social and intellectual proscription of which he had been, and still was, a victim. By 1878 he had decided that stenography would be the magic carpet to whisk his family to the "land of opportunity," and set about improving his self-taught shorthand until he could take 200 words a minute. Such proficiency, Chesnutt believed, would guarantee his employment in the North. Whenever he had a spare moment, he practiced shorthand instead of writing stories.[29]

CHAPTER 2

Weaving the Magic Carpet

I occupy here [in the South] a position similar to that of Mahomet's Coffin. I am neither fish, flesh, nor fowl—neither "nigger," white, nor "buckrah." Too "stuck-up" for the colored folks, and, of course, not recognized by the whites. Now these things I imagine I would escape from, in some degree, if I lived in the North. The colored people would be more intelligent, and the white people less prejudiced; so that if I did not reach *terra firma*, I would at least be in sight of land on either side.[1]

NO one will ever know the full extent of the "social and intellectual proscription" which Chesnutt suffered in the South. His journals, however, give moving evidence that his psyche was repeatedly scarred by both deliberate and unintentional acts of discrimination against him. Each act thrust him further into the void between the acclaimed egalitarian creed of his country and the countervailing deeds of its citizens.

I *Race and Color Bars*

Some of the more traumatic incidents, recorded while still pain-bright in Chesnutt's memory, are important. They not only provide a better understanding of his didactic bent—as enunciated in his purpose for writing—but also show how much Chesnutt, for fictional purposes, drew upon his own experiences, which were also the experiences of other Afro-Americans of his time. Moreover, Chesnutt was an outsider, with the special problems which plague persons of such mixed ancestry that their appearance often belies their legal ethnic identity in a country where color seemed to outweigh character.

The situations ranged from comic to tragic, and Chesnutt, who identified with blacks but could not be distinguished from a Caucasian, ran the gamut. Once, while seeking a summer teaching position, he ran into prejudice at opposite ends of the color line. During an interview with rural North Carolina school board members, "the blackest colored people" he had ever seen, Chesnutt noticed their bias against a little eight-year-old girl "because she was yellow."[2] In another small settlement he asked for a colored school, but was offered the white one with the warning that white people would not respect him if he took a colored school. Though Chesnutt had no other job prospect, he "respectfully declined." The paradox of the racial situation insofar as he was concerned is contained in an old white man's observation recorded at the time by Chesnutt: " 'Look here, Tom, here's a black fellow as white as you air.' "[3]

Chesnutt's Caucasian features notwithstanding, educational, cultural, and political doors in Fayetteville were closed to him because of his ethnic identity. But for the intercession of Dr. T. D. Haigh, the Chesnutt family physician, and the empathy of Prof. E. N. Neufeld, a foreign Jew, Chesnutt would have been unable to engage Neufeld to tutor him in French and German. Further, though Chesnutt appreciated good music, he complained, "I never hear what little there is to be heard." Again, after Chesnutt reluctantly accepted the Republican nomination for town commissioner in 1880, he observed wryly that white friends put "so 'many fleas in my ear' that I sent in my formal withdrawal to the chairman . . . and backed off as gracefully as possible."[4] Even George Haigh, who ten years earlier had given young Charles the run of his bookstore, insisted to the adult Chesnutt "that this fretting about one's condition was fighting against God's will . . . a man who doesn't like [the status quo should] go where things are different."[5]

In 1881 "a poor-white" clerk in a Fayetteville store concluded a discussion with a freedman about Chesnutt's obvious merits as a "perfect gentleman in every respect," by stating with finality, "Well, he's a nigger; and with me a nigger is a nigger, and nothing in the world can make him anything else but a nigger." By this time Chesnutt was convinced that this declaration embodied "the opinion of the South on the 'Negro Question.' "[6] Spurred by the constant rebuffs, he made an unsuccessful attempt in May 1879 to secure employment as a court reporter in Washington, D. C. The trip was beneficial, nevertheless. Chesnutt found out how much he needed to improve his stenographic skills, toured the national capital, and en route home observed some rollicking Negro farm workers who were the genesis of a similar group in his second novel, *The Marrow of Tradition*.

II *Northward Bound*

During the next four years, intrigued by the exciting promise of the North and disillusioned by increasing racial strictures in the South, Chesnutt gradually attained the proficiency in shorthand which would command a job in the "promised land." By May 1883 he could take the required 200 words a minute. He thereupon submitted his resignation as principal of the Normal School despite the dismay of family, friends, and the general community. He knew that his professional success was assured in Fayetteville, but he could not trade that for "civilization" and "equality." Nor did an unprecedented offer of $85 a month [7] weaken his resolve to "go to the North, where, although the prejudice sticks . . . yet a man may enjoy . . . privileges if he has the money to pay for them."[8] He left North Carolina, but North Carolina never left him. In his heart as well as in his journals Chesnutt carried the germinal ideas for the bulk and the best of the writing which enabled him to realize his dream of becoming an author.

Chesnutt went first to New York. But within six months his own acute loneliness and the conviction that it was not the best place to rear children—including the "rosy" little Neddie, born after Chesnutt had left Fayetteville—prompted his move to Cleveland. There he had relatives and friends. He soon secured a position writing letters and footing ledgers in the accounting department of the Nickel Plate Railroad Company. By April he had saved enough money to rent a little house, to furnish it with "the barest necessities," and to send railroad fare for his family.[9] Happily, the warmth of the family reunion and of friendly neighbors helped the newcomers to overcome initial misgivings and to think of Cleveland as home. And home it remained through remarkably productive, prosperous years that brought Chesnutt respect as a citizen and recognition as a writer.

In the meantime the beginning author worked hard at business in order to have more leisure to devote to the pleasurable avocation of writing. Within a year he was transferred to the legal department of the Nickel Plate, where for two years he served as a stenographer and studied law in the office of Judge Samuel E. Williamson. In addition, in the evenings the energetic young man tried his hand at writing and rewriting very short sketches of real or imagined occurrences which might have popular appeal.

In spite of these activities, Chesnutt found time to enjoy his family. His daughter Helen recalled him as a father with a very keen sense of humor who often told or read the children stories by Defoe, Swift, Sir Walter Scott, Dickens, Mark Twain, and George W. Cable—all favorite Chesnutt authors. His own writing got off to a very slow start, marked by rejection slips which began arriving as early as 1882. In 1885 and thereafter, however, he found a market for a number of his anecdotes and tales in the newspapers comprising the McClure Syndicate, and in *Family Fiction: The Great International Story Weekly*, *Puck*, and *Tid-Bits*. Chesnutt received only five or ten dollars for each piece; his chief reward was in seeing his name in print, as when his first story of substance, "Uncle Peter's House," appeared in the *Cleveland News and Herald* in December 1885.

After Chesnutt passed the Ohio bar in 1887 with the highest grades in his group, Judge Williamson asked about his plans for the future. Upon learning that Chesnutt was seriously considering moving to Europe, where he might be able both to earn a living professionally and to "relieve his children of certain disabilities inevitable in the United States," the judge offered to advance money for the voyage and for living expenses until Chesnutt could become established. After discussing the matter with Susan, he decided to try to gain recognition "as a scholar and a gentleman" in his own country; he felt that such success would be more meaningful. That same year the *Atlantic Monthly* published his "The Goophered Grapevine." This is believed to be the first fiction by an Afro-American to appear in the most prestigious magazine of the period, although Chesnutt's ethnic identity was not publicized until 1899. A second conjure tale, "Po' Sandy," published in the *Atlantic* the following April, brought the fledgling writer to the attention of George Washington Cable, with whom he shared sociological as well as literary interests. At last Chesnutt was on the way to realize his long-cherished dream of becoming a recognized writer.

CHAPTER 3

Business for Pleasure

Every time I read a good novel, I want to write one. It is the dream of my life—to be an author! It is not so much the *monstraci digito*, though that has something to do with my aspirations. It is not altogether the money. It is a mixture of motives. I want fame; I want money; I want to raise my children in a different rank of life from that I sprang from. . . . But literature pays the successful. There is a fascination about this calling that draws a scribbler irresistibly toward his doom. He knows the chance of success is hardly one out of a hundred; but he is foolish enough to believe or sanguine enough to hope, that he will be the successful one.[1]

I *Literary Background*

CHARLES W. Chesnutt had to become a writer. Some powerful inner compulsion compensated for the culturally arid atmosphere of his formative years and the dearth of intellectually stimulating exchange before he moved back to Cleveland. For one to admit during the 1870s and early 1880s the possibility of Chesnutt's ever satisfying his obsessive desire to write, expressed repeatedly in early journal entries, seemed an affront to reality. His main access to the world of letters was through a limited number of books and periodicals, most of which concerned British and Continental masters and a sprinkling of the few American writers—none with African antecedents—whom an educated gentleman of the times would be expected to know. Thus Chesnutt, like most American authors before him, was initially inspired more by British and European than by black or white American writers.

Whether Chesnutt read many Afro-American authors while he lived in Fayetteville has not been determined. However, infrequent references to them in his journals and speeches through 1883 suggest that relatively few of the substantial body of writings by blacks between 1746 and 1883 filtered down to Fayetteville. In one such passage Chesnutt is highly critical of the

work of black writers he had read by early 1881. After skimming
William Wells Brown's *The Negro in the American Rebellion: His
Heroism and His Fidelity* (1867), he noted that "Dr. Brown's
books are mere compilations. . . . If they were not written by a
colored man they would not sell for enough to pay for the
printing."[2]

Chesnutt's sweeping condemnation of the literary efforts of his
fellow blacks had two probable causes. One could have been his
not having read the more important writers among them. The
other was quite likely his awareness and resentment of the
patronizing attitude of editors, publishers, and critics, an attitude
by which they justified their setting lower literary standards for
authors known to be black. After Chesnutt was published in the
Atlantic, he reconfirmed his position by declaring he would not
have a proposed book "judged by any standard lower than that
set for other writers."[3]

Impelled by such attitudes as well as by his personal aspirations, Chesnutt strove to excel. He considered second-class
literary goals as unworthy as the second-class status which increasingly impeded his people. He wanted to write stories which
would hasten the coming of the time when the United States
would actually be a democracy. He expressed the urgency of his
feelings in a letter to Cable on March 28, 1890:

It is easy enough to temporize with the bull when you are on the other side
of the fence, but when you are in the pasture with him as the colored
people of the South are, the case is different. I take it that every citizen is
entitled to such protection as the government can extend to him in the en-
joyment of his rights, and that he is entitled to that protection now, and
whenever his rights are invaded. I sincerely hope the present Congress
will pass a wise and practicable federal elections law, and that the President [Benjamin Harrison] will have brains enough and backbone enough
to enforce it. The ever-lengthening record of Southern wrongs and insults,
both lawless and under the form of law, calls for whatever there is of
patriotism, of justice, of fair play in the American people, to cry hands off
and give the Negro a show, not five years hence or 10 years hence, or a
generation hence, but now while he is alive, and can appreciate it;
posthumous fame is a glorious thing, even if it is only posthumous;
posthumous liberty is not, in the homely language of the rural Southerner,
"wuth shucks."[4]

Chesnutt knew that he would have to meet high literary standards and strongly appeal to popular taste if he wished to win

critical approbation as an author and to promote a successful moral revolution in black-white relations in the United States. The following chronological survey of his work traces Chesnutt's course of action in seeking to achieve these personal and social objectives, and identifies major forces which either helped or hindered him. When Chesnutt began to write in earnest during the early 1880s, he concentrated on very short fiction: anecdote, tall tale, fantasy, and sketch. In these he either avoided or treated only tangentially the controversial issues, based upon the doctrine of equal rights, which became the themes of his later folk tales, stories, novels, and essays.

II *First Fruits*

By 1891 Chesnutt had published at least sixteen pieces of short fiction on conventional subjects approved by the editors of *Family Fiction, Puck, Tid-Bits, Youth's Companion*, and the McClure Syndicate. Most of the characters are white. This feature removed a possible obstacle to publication, for, as Chesnutt's later correspondence indicates, publishers limited the number of stories with Negro characters they would accept.[5] But Chesnutt had another reason as well; he was saving what he considered his best material, treating mostly black characters, for the time when he had gained more skill and some stature as a writer. All of his subsequent fiction except *The Colonel's Dream* has a preponderance of Afro-American characters, and his nonfiction treats matters important to them.

Chesnutt's early published productions are more often humorous—at least on the surface. His anecdotes and tall tales, with all the brusque, bungling bite of old Southwest humor, are usually true to life and revelatory of character. The anecdotal "A Soulless Corporation" (1887) is illustrative. Ironic from title to end, this amusing account shows the grasping Mrs. Lovelock trying to collect from a railroad company $200 damage for a trunk shown subsequently to be worth only $1.50 and not even her own.[6]

Many other pieces also have autobiographical overtones. "McDugald's Mule" (1887) falls in the tall tale category and harks back to the North Carolina of Chesnutt's youth. Dugald McDugald, a white sandhills farmer, explains to "Cholly" (no doubt young Charles) at the general store (probably the Chesnutt grocery) why McDugald indulges his mule's stubbornness. One day on a trip to Lumberton, no amount of cajoling, threatening, or coercion could make Beauregard approach an old wooden bridge over the swollen Lumber River. Another man, who started over the bridge in a horse-drawn "kyart," drowned when the structure buckled and collapsed. Thereafter McDugald and his son "never hendered [*sic*] that mule from having his own way."

The short fantasies are both spoofing and sentimental. In "The Origin of the Hatchet Story," the narrator questions the originality of George Washington's cherry tree legend through the disclosure of the antics of an ancient Egyptian prince in papyrus records he comes upon during a trip abroad. On the other hand, "A Secret Ally" shows nostalgically how Colonel Brierson's dream about his youthful transgressions influences him to approve of his son's marrying a girl of a lower social class. Each is gently critical of human flaws.

Thus most of the author's earlier adult publications concern blacks and whites in largely noncontroversial situations and relationships. "Uncle Peter's House" (1885) is an exception. An old couple, recently freed from slavery, are forced by young white perpetrators to witness the burning of the modest little home in which all their savings are invested. Undaunted, they try to replace it. Unfortunately, the old man dies of injuries he sustains in the rebuilding process. Except for its extreme pathos, the narrative foreshadows Chesnutt's subsequent writings, especially those set in the South.

The Uncle Julius tales, Chesnutt's most popular literary efforts, are set in the Fayetteville of his childhood and hark back to "days befo' de Wah." Clearly superior in both form and content to Chesnutt's previous published fiction, these tales illustrate his shift of focus from the earlier, lighter pieces to the more serious works upon which he concentrated after 1890. The first of these, "The Goophered Grapevine" (*Atlantic*, August 1887), a deceptively simple folktale in the Joel Chandler Harris manner, covertly criticizes heartless, dishonest commerce in human beings. According to Hugh M. Gloster, this initial appearance of a work, and later stories, by a black man in the best literary magazine of the period marked the coming of age of Negro literature in the United States.[7] The achievement was not noted at the time; a desire for his creative efforts to be judged solely on the basis of their literary merit led Chesnutt to omit any mention of his ethnic identity when he submitted this "conjure" story. Further, Chesnutt wrote with such objectivity that most of his readers, including the critics, assumed that he was white. Though he voluntarily revealed his antecedents to Houghton Mifflin in September 1891, his publishers maintained a discreet silence on the matter until reviewer Carolyn Shipman and an anonymous columnist indicated his racial identity in the *Critic* in July 1899.[8] As for being black, Chesnutt later declared, "It never occurred to me to claim merit because of it, and I have always resented the denial of anything on account of it."[9]

By the time "Po' Sandy" (on the tragic outcome of repeated separation of slave husband and wife) appeared in the *Atlantic* and "The Sheriff's Children" (the first of his shocking color-line stories to be published) in the *Independent* in November 1889, Chesnutt had received praise as a writer from many people, including Albion W. Tourgée and George W. Cable. These two well-known authors, already aware of Chesnutt's "African descent," had both lived in and written about the South. Tourgée migrated to North Carolina from Ohio after the Civil War; Cable was a native of Louisiana. Their liberal views on "The Negro Question" aroused such hostility that both subsequently moved north of the Mason-Dixon line. The three men had much in common: concern about minority groups, especially blacks; belief that literature should have ethical purposes; preference for familiar southern settings (North Carolina, for example, by both Tourgée and Chesnutt); treatment of the recent past or the present; reading from their fiction on the lyceum circuit; and use of letters, essays, and lectures as well as fiction to present their views on current issues.

In a letter to Chesnutt dated December 8, 1888, Tourgée compliments him on his writing and voices his belief that Chesnutt "will do much to solve the great question of the hour—the greatest question of the world's history—the future of the Negro man in America."[10] He also predicted, correctly, that the black man would achieve fame in literature sooner than in politics.

Chesnutt was also corresponding with Cable. In a letter written sometime during March 1889 Chesnutt detailed his literary virtuosity, declaring, "I can turn my hand to several kinds of literary work, can write a story, a funny skit, can turn a verse, and write a serious essay. I have even written a novel, though it has never seen the light, nor been offered to a publisher." He explained that he was motivated by "a deep and growing interest in the discussion and settlement of the Southern question, and all other questions which affect the happiness of the millions of colored people in this country" and elsewhere in the world. These people, Chesnutt felt, would make good subject matter for one tied to them by blood and sympathy.[11]

Both Tourgée and Cable encouraged Chesnutt to continue writing. Cable, later called Chesnutt's mentor, offered much helpful advice. Fortunately, Chesnutt ignored Cable's admonition not to "found fiction on fact"; his meticulously correct depiction of the conditions of his time enhances his value as a social historian. On the other hand, Cable's tempered criticism and that of Walter Hines Page later helped Chesnutt to write better fiction. In addition, these humanitarians encouraged Chesnutt to continue expressing his decided views on various aspects of race relations in essay as well as in fictional form at a time when most white Americans ignored the Afro-American side of the race question.

In turn, Cable and Tourgée asked for Chesnutt's assistance in carrying out special projects of their own to promote better race relations. Early in 1889, when Chesnutt thought official stenographers were going to be employed in Cuyahoga County, Ohio, courts instead of independent reporting services such as he operated, he sought Cable's advice on securing a position which would afford him a modest income and also leave him some time for writing. After an interview at Northampton, Cable invited Chesnutt to become his secretary. Much of the work concerned the shortlived Open Letter Club, which provided "a medium for the interchange of information of every sort and from every direction, valuable to the moral, intellectual, and material interests of the South."[12] The annual salary offered, possibly $1,200 to $1,500, was less than half the income anticipated from the firm Chesnutt had expanded after the county government had decided to continue using private services. Indicating that the financial sacrifice would be unfair to his family, Chesnutt regretfully declined the offer. At the same time, however, he offered his services from Cleveland gratis "to still do what I can in the good cause of human rights."[13] Thereafter, until Cable dissolved the club in 1890, Chesnutt, the only Afro-American member, provided names for the mailing list, submitted essays—including "An Inside View of the Negro Question"—extracted and analyzed materials submitted by others, and collected requested data on subjects such as Negro education in the South, Negro rights, and North Carolina government. Early in November 1889, while on a western lecture tour, Cable visited the Chesnutts in their newly built house at 64 Brenton Street. During that visit Chesnutt promised to send to Cable, for distribution through the Open Letter Club, reports showing the disproportionate amounts allocated to Negro schools.

In 1893 Tourgée asked Chesnutt to become associate editor of and to buy $2,500 worth of stock in the *National Citizen*, a magazine which Tourgée proposed to edit and publish. It was to be concerned exclusively with Negro rights. Chesnutt bought only one share; besides being unable to invest the requested sum, he feared that the periodical would not sell. He had already found out that among "the best white people of one of the most advanced communities of the United States [Cleveland, Ohio] the wrongs of the Negro" were unpopular subjects of conversation.[14]

Despite having been heartened since 1887 by the warm reception given to his treatment of the old-time Negroes (including mulattoes)—in some ways like characterizations by Harris, Harry Stillwell Edwards, Thomas Nelson Page, and Cable—Chesnutt continued to have difficulty placing stories featuring other types.[15] Stories with Afro-American characters, however, constantly posed special publication problems for the author, especially as the novelty of the material wore off near the end of the nineteenth century. Walter Hines Page, acting for the *Atlantic*, early in February 1897 accepted "The Wife of His Youth" and "The March of Progress," later exchanged for "A Matter of Principle."[16] All three stories show less typical blacks coping with color or race prejudice. Later that year, however, Page turned down three others treating black-white relations because the *Atlantic* editors had "had such hard luck in making room for [Chesnutt's] other two stories."[17]

"The Wife of His Youth" (*Atlantic*, July 1898) was the first piece of Chesnutt's fiction to receive serious critical and widespread public attention. In it a now prosperous and cultivated freeman acknowledges his unattractive, illiterate ex-slave wife despite their long separation and his previous intent to marry an educated, cultivated widow. The generally favorable reaction to this short story, unique in its treatment of "the color line" and class among Negroes, accurately forecast the reception by literary critics of the two collections of short stories, a brief biography of Frederick Douglass, and three novels published between 1899 and 1905. Reading "The Wife of His Youth" moved author James Lane Allen to write Page on June 27, 1898: "Who—in the name of the Lord!—is Charles W. Chesnutt?" Calling the story "the freshest, finest, most admirably held in and wrought out little story that has gladdened—and moistened—my eyes in many months," Allen sent his thanks and his blessings to Chesnutt.[18]

Chesnutt emerged from literary obscurity at a time when he had become almost convinced, by rejection of his more serious stories and by deteriorating race relations in the United States, that he would have to make his "literary *debut* on the other side of the Atlantic."[19] But Page, in taking Chesnutt's material for the *Atlantic*, had encouraged the writer of "one of the best short stories of the year" to offer a collection of his stories to Houghton Mifflin and to submit his novel when it was ready. When the collection was accepted, Chesnutt, again hopeful of winning recognition in the United States without violating his avowed purpose for becoming an author, decided against moving to England.

By devoting most of his free time thereafter in 1898 and from 1902 to 1905 to his literary career (between 1899 and 1901, he closed his stenographic service in order to write full time), Chesnutt saw in print the bulk of his work published during his lifetime. These consisted of two collections of short stories, *The Conjure Woman* (1899) and *The Wife of His Youth and Other Stories of the Color Line* (1899); a biography, *Frederick Douglass* (1899); three novels: *The House Behind the Cedars* (1900), *The Marrow of Tradition* (1901), and *The Colonel's Dream* (1905); a number of short stories published separately; and more than a dozen essays in books and periodicals. In addition, Chesnutt continued his practice of writing letters and making speeches about contemporary conditions and issues.

III *Major Works*

A. The Conjure Woman

The first collection, *The Conjure Woman* (1899), contains seven pre–Civil War folk tales. They are told by wily Uncle Julius

McAdoo to his new employers, a northern couple who have
decided to buy and live on the old plantation near Patesville,
North Carolina, where Julius was once a slave. Chesnutt follows
the practice of many southern humorists in his use of the framing
device to connect the stories. Written largely in the local Negro
dialect, most of the tales depend upon a particular kind of Afro-
American folk magic known as "conjure." They also depict blacks
with the basic motivations and responses common to mankind
rather than the unnaturally self-abnegating or ridiculously stupid
stereotypes that Chesnutt detested. In a letter to Walter Hines
Page dated March 22, 1899, Chesnutt referred to Harry Stillwell
Edwards's "Chief," a caricature of the devoted ex-slave which appeared in that month's issue of the *Atlantic*, as "one of the sort of
Southern stories that make me feel it my duty to try to write a different sort."[20]

The careful reader discerns that Chesnutt's Uncle Julius,
although seemingly in the less offensive Joel Chandler Harris
tradition, is more self-serving than altruistic.[21] Uncle Julius in-
variably chooses a tale not only to entertain his employers, John
and Miss Annie, but also to move them—especially the
tenderhearted, superstitious wife—to follow the advice which
leads to an end Julius has predetermined. Chesnutt wrote at least
seven other Uncle Julius tales.

In eight of the stories either "Aun' Peggy," the conjure woman,
who is also the chief unifying element of this group, or Uncle
Jube, an older and more powerful conjure man, uses thauma-
turgic powers to correct conditions which are beyond the ability
of ordinary people to change. John, who introduces all the tales,
observes in "Po' Sandy" that "some of these stories are quaintly
humorous; others wildly extravagant, revealing the Oriental cast
of the Negro's imagination; while others . . . disclose many a
tragic incident of the darker side of slavery."[22] For example, "Po'
Sandy," "Sis' Becky's Pickaninny," "Lonesome Ben," and "Hot-
Foot Hannibal" show the sometimes agonizing pain suffered by
separated slave families or sweethearts. "The Conjurer's Revenge," "The Gray Wolf's Ha'nt," and "The Marked Tree" reflect
the strong motivating power of love, jealousy, and revenge,
whether those affected are slave or free. "The Goophered
Grapevine" reveals deliberate fraud in slave trading and "Dave's
Neckliss" a callous indifference to slave integrity. "Mars Jeems's

Nightmare" catalogues all the evils of the slave system, but emphasizes brutal treatment.

As Chesnutt intended, these tales, in a format already pleasantly familiar to the public, present slave life from the victims' more traumatized point of view. Even so, the treatment is so objective and/or ironic that many readers remained as unaware of Chesnutt's implicit purpose as Miss Annie does of Julius's aims. The overall response to this book in the United States, England, and Australia identified Chesnutt as one of the outstanding short-story writers of his time; he achieved a literary preeminence unmatched by any Afro-American prose writer before him and equaled only in poetry by his contemporary, Paul Laurence Dunbar. Thus, by coating didacticism with the appeal of the familiar and offering it with generous portions of local color, humor, and pathos, Chesnutt was initially successful in achieving, in part, his "high and holy purpose" for writing.

B. Frederick Douglass

Between the publication of *The Conjure Woman* and his next collection of short stories, Chesnutt prepared a brief but excellent biography of Frederick Douglass as requested by the editors of Small, Maynard & Company for inclusion in its "Beacon Biographies of Eminent Americans." Chesnutt brought to his task a profound personal sympathy and the special admiration he reserved for black men of achievement. However, given the space limitations imposed upon him, Chesnutt felt that he could only "touch upon the salient features of [Douglass's] career . . . suggest the respects in which [Douglass] influenced the course of events in his lifetime, and . . . epitomize for the readers of another generation the judgment of his contemporaries as to his genius and his character."[23]

C. The Wife of His Youth and Other Stories of the Color Line

The Wife of His Youth and Other Stories of the Color Line, also published by Houghton Mifflin, went on sale in December 1899. The selections are more contemporary and more serious in tone than the tales in *The Conjure Woman*: Chesnutt's purpose in these stories and several others in the same vein was to focus attention on "certain aspects of the race question which are quite familiar to those on the unfortunate side of it," but unknown or ignored by others.[24] These aspects reflect less concern about the well-defined pre–Civil War plantation hierarchies than about the more complex relationships of blacks and whites after Emancipation. The Afro-American characters range in color from black to white; in condition, from sophisticated Northern urban affluence to naive Southern rural poverty. Chesnutt exposes and castigates the color or class bias, which knows no Mason-Dixon line, expressed in acts of discrimination and injustice both between and within racial groups. In "The Wife of His Youth" and "A Matter of Principle," Chesnutt satirizes the color complexes of the Groveland, Ohio, Negroes banded together as the Blue Veins.[25] The tragic results of miscegenation unfold in "The Sheriff's Children" and "Her Virginia Mammy." However, in the latter Chesnutt forecasts greater black-white marital success than either Cable or Howells does. "Uncle Wellington's Wives" suggests why mulatto Uncle Wellington's shortlived marriage to an Irish cook and washerwoman in the North fails. In "The Passing of Grandison," a slave outwits owners falsely secure in their feelings of racial superiority and leads his family to freedom via the Underground Railroad. Neither race nor color is a determining factor in the blasting of "Cicely's Dream," but "The Bouquet" and "The Web of Circumstance," the concluding selections, are moving revelations of the harmful—sometimes fatal—results of discrimination and injustice between and within black and white ethnic groups.

D. The House Behind the Cedars

This theme is explored more fully in *The House Behind the Cedars*, initially serialized in *Self-Culture*, later *Modern Culture* (August 1900 through February 1901), and published by Houghton Mifflin in 1900. Pre–Civil War prohibition of interracial marriage in North Carolina results in miscegenation and the loss of patrimony for John and Rowena (Rena) Walden, the two octoroon offspring of "Mis' Molly Walden," a mulatto, upon the sudden death of their father. John, the elder, unwilling to be hampered by his legal identity as a Negro in his home state, migrates to South Carolina and becomes successful as John Warwick, a white man. Complications arise when he persuades his mother to let Rena reap the benefits of "passing" by going to live with him. Within a year, schooled and groomed, the girl wins complete acceptance in her new life, but does not make a clean break with her old one. George Tryon, Warwick's best friend, falls in love with Rowena, who reciprocates. Disclosure of her racial identity to Tryon causes him to reject her. His vacillating behavior thereafter and the unwelcome attentions of licentious mulatto Jeff Wain result in Rowena's tragic death despite the altruistic efforts of Frank Fowler to help her. Mis' Molly and her friends, less cultured counterparts of the Northern Blue Veins, show similar color prejudice in their relations with darker Negroes, especially Fowler, who emerges finally as Rena's best friend. This work, altogether serious in tone and subject matter, marks Chesnutt's move completely into the second stage of his planned campaign against caste in the United States.

E. The Marrow of Tradition

Chesnutt's next novel, *The Marrow of Tradition* (1901), is an explosive expression of the disappointment, resentment, and alarm he and most other blacks in the United States were feeling at the accelerating decline in their status since the end of the Civil War—extralegally in the 1860s and legally in the 1870s and thereafter. As a result of a pronounced southern Negro psychosis which also affected northern attitudes, Afro-Americans were stringently proscribed in their attempts to participate as equals in any aspect of community life. The concepts of white supremacy and second class citizenship defined the limits of acceptable interaction between blacks and whites.[26]

Chesnutt was especially disappointed in North Carolina, which in 1879 he had praised as exemplary.[27] Reacting particularly to blatant appeals to race hate during "the 'White Supremacy' Campaign" which ended on November 4, 1898, with the election of an all-white slate, on November 10 Chesnutt wrote Walter Hines Page that he felt obliged to revise some of his judgments:

There is absolutely no excuse for the state of things there, for the State has a very large white majority. It is an outbreak of pure malignant and altogether indefensible race prejudice, which makes me feel personally humiliated and ashamed for the country and the State. The United States

Government is apparently powerless, and the recent occurrences in Illinois in connection with the miners' strike seem to emphasize its weakness.[28]

On the same day—though Chesnutt was then unaware of the appropriateness of his appraisal—the Wilmington (North Carolina) Riot was taking place. An Afro-American newspaper office was ransacked and the building set on fire by a mob of about "600 armed white citizens" who then "shot up the Negro district." During this rampage they destroyed other property, killed a number of blacks outright (estimates range from eleven to more than 100), caused a mass flight of others to nearby woods, and forced "bumptious negro political leaders" and officials of both races—most of whose terms were expiring—to resign posthaste and leave town immediately and permanently.[29]

Accounts of the seemingly pointless violence in the news media and by witnesses, many of whom were Chesnutt's close relatives and friends, outraged the author. That incident in particular and post-1890 race relations in general inspired *The Marrow of Tradition*. In a letter of November 4, 1901, to the Reverend Dr. I. B. Scott, editor of the *Southwestern Christian Advocate*, Chesnutt described it as "both a novel and a political and sociological tract—a tremendous combination if the author can but find the formula for mixing them."[30] The book explores the personal and professional relationships of the families of Dr. William Miller, an Afro-American surgeon who had done postgraduate study in Vienna, and that of the aristocratic white Major Philip Carteret, owner-editor of the local newspaper. Miller and most of the other blacks attempt futilely to achieve self-realization and self-determination by following the Puritan work ethic; Carteret and his associates manipulate the power structure to maintain the status quo. That the wives of these men are legal half-sisters and that the fate of the only child of each couple is determined by the group interaction lends an additional twist to the suspenseful plot. Another subplot about a robbery and murder involves three white aristocrats and an ex-slave servant. The denouement reflects Chesnutt's realistic assessment of the viable alternative responses to racism available to a professional black man at that time. In the outcome the blacks are the moral victors, but the whites give no indication that they will be any more fair on race matters now that they completely control the city.

The Marrow of Tradition is Chesnutt's most fiery and documentary novel. He painstakingly gathered data for it while on a lecture and fact-finding tour of several southern states in February 1901. The extent of his personal commitment is suggested in his letter of November 11, 1905, to Mrs. W. E. Henderson, whose husband, an attorney, was among the prominent citizens who had to flee Wilmington:

I share the blood of the race, I lived in North Carolina from the age of 9 to that of 25; I taught school there for ten years; three of my children were born there, and many of my relations, including some of the nearest and dearest, are living there still. I could never be so placed in life that I should not have an abiding interest in the welfare of our people in the South.[31]

As with his other books, Chesnutt had more than a personal or literary concern in writing this novel: what he had seen of race relations in the South had depressed him greatly. Some of his impressions, recorded while still fresh, are given in "The White and the Black," treating Atlanta University, higher education for Negroes, and southern segregation laws, in the *Boston Transcript*, March 20, 1901; and "A Visit to Tuskegee," in the *Cleveland Leader* of March 31, 1901.[32] Chesnutt found even more offensive than the vicious antiblack attitude of whites the libelous *The American Negro*, by a Negro, William Hannibal Thomas. White editorial readers, largely unacquainted with the Afro-American culture and totally unaware of Thomas's unsavory reputation, had approved the book for publication by Macmillan. Primarily through the efforts of Chesnutt in letters to the publisher and in the columns of the *Transcript* and the *Critic*, Macmillan withdrew the book from the market.[33]

The failure of *The House Behind the Cedars*, which had won critical approval, to sell as expected clearly indicated to Chesnutt that his choice and treatment of subject matter were too controversial for the general reading public. He should have realized that the likelihood of maintaining his financial solvency or increasing his literary popularity would be lessened by the militancy in *The Marrow of Tradition*. But he clung to the belief that the book could shock white America out of its indifference to the desperate plight of the Negro in the South, especially his disfranchisement.

Chesnutt continued to write narratives as well as essays and letters. In "Baxter's Procrustes," published in the *Atlantic* in June 1904, he demonstrated more impressively than ever before his mastery of the short-story form. Freed temporarily from the assumed obligation of helping his fellow blacks become first-class citizens, Chesnutt suggests in this *jeu d'esprit* his artistic potential.[34] Using affluent white characters as members of a book-lovers club obviously inspired by the exclusive Rowfant Club of Cleveland, Chesnutt gently but pointedly satirizes their preoccupation with the embellishments of rather than the ideas in their precious books.

F. The Colonel's Dream

While "Baxter's Procrustes" was provoking knowing smiles in Cleveland's inner circles and appreciative chuckles from readers everywhere, Walter Hines Page, by now a partner with Double-day Page in New York, was encouraging Chesnutt to expand a shorter version of what became *The Colonel's Dream* for publication by that firm. Houghton Mifflin had already regretfully declined to bring out the novel, which they thought better than *The Marrow of Tradition*, because of the financial losses they had incurred in publishing both the latter work and *The House Behind the Cedars*. Apparently the editors doubted that Chesnutt could "write a book dealing with the color line from [his] point of view which would be likely to make a popular success . . . [either] enough to produce a modest return from the amount expended in writing it" or in publishing it. Chesnutt's principal aim in writing had never been to make money, but "an ethical purpose entirely apart from that"; yet he realized that unless his books were widely read he would not be able to achieve even his ethical end.[35]

Chesnutt was apprehensive about falling into obvious didacticism in treating race relations, for he realized that preaching was not art. Having been thoroughly discouraged by the slow sale of his other novels on that theme and encouraged by friends to try other subjects, he had "almost decided to foreswear [*sic*] the race problem stories, but [wanted to write—like Turgenev and Tolstoy—] a good one which would be widely read, before [he] quit."[36] *The Colonel's Dream* (1905) is also a novel with a purpose, that of bringing "the forces of enlightenment to bear upon the vexed problems which harass the South . . . ," but less impassioned than *The Marrow of Tradition*. That Chesnutt did not see racial discord as the cause of all those problems is emphasized by the absence of major Negro characters from the book. Rather, he was concerned about weighty social issues as they affected every American of his day.

The plot development reflects Chesnutt's conviction that the best answers for such questions are most likely to be found when "we treat individuals as individuals."[37] The protagonist, Col. Henry French, is ideally suited to follow this line of action when he returns to his home town of Clarendon to "build up the waste places, to heal the wounds of slavery and of war." French is a southern-bred aristocrat, a Civil War veteran, a successful businessman, and a kind father and friend. Nevertheless, he offends working class whites by his color-blind business practices; he loses his fiancée, the aristocratic Miss Laura Treadwell, because of basic differences in their attitudes, especially toward blacks; he uncovers but cannot stop an illegal, highly profitable traffic in convict labor being conducted by public officials and the local business magnate, William Fetters, who also owns cotton mills where conditions for the white labor force are deplorable. Thus disappointed and also losing both his son and an old servant in a freak accident, French returns to the North and a new life. Of the major characters, only young Graciella Treadwell and Ben Dudley show any likelihood of positive change, which, if achieved, will hardly affect the racial status quo.

The future had brought worse rather than better times to the Afro-American. The racial atmosphere created by the continuing decline in the status of blacks and a corresponding upsurge in racism probably helped to make *The Colonel's Dream* the least popular of Chesnutt's novels, despite the mildness of its tone and the subordination of certain delicate aspects of race relations which in other works had antagonized many readers in whom Chesnutt had hoped to "create sympathy throughout the country for our cause." The most reactionary of the southern writers, the Reverend Thomas Dixon, was apparently more in tune with the times. He had been lionized by whites upon the publication of *The Leopard's Spots* in 1902 and gained additional popularity with the appearance of two other novels, *The Clansman* (1905) and *The Traitor: A Story of the Fall of the Invisible Empire* (1907). Dixon's trilogy offers a consistently sensational characterization of the Negro as beastly. In the same vein, Thomas Nelson Page was no longer content to keep the Negro in his inconsequential place as the contented slave in his fiction; in the expository *The Negro: The Southerner's Problem* (1904), he denies that "the Negro is the equal of the white, or ever could be." Page declares further that the Afro-American has no sense of morality and is incapable of self-direction.[38] Neither of these men was unique in his portrayal of the Negro.

IV *Letters, Essays, and Activity*

In the meantime, Chesnutt gave up neither writing nor fighting for Afro-Americans. During his tour of the South in 1901 he had been greatly impressed by Tuskegee and had begun a lasting friendship with its founder, Booker T. Washington. Despite warm mutual admiration, however, they were unable to reconcile some differences in their philosophies on race relations. Chesnutt disapproved of Washington's emphasis upon industrial education at the expense of higher education for the Negro. He thought attempting to win the friendship of the white South at any cost was foolhardy; he was also convinced that securing and safeguarding the southern Negro's civil and political rights were prerequisite for his economic well-being. The two men exchanged many letters on this subject. In one dated January 1, 1908, Chesnutt argued:

As to the ballot, the importance of a thing is not to be measured by the number of times you do it. Some of the most important & vital things of life are done only once. . . . The importance of the ballot is to me a paramount element of citizenship. A man can earn his daily bread easier and bank more money with it than without it. You argue the question as though the Negro must choose between voting & eating. He ought to do both, and he can do both better together than he can do either alone. It is not the *act* of voting I speak of—it is the right of every citizen to have some part in the choice of those who rule him, and the only way he can express that choice is at the polls. It is just as effective if he votes once in five years as once a day. Would you maintain for a moment that the economic conditions in the South, which crush the Negro & drive away white immigration, would continue to exist if the Negroes could vote, and their votes were directed by intelligent leadership? If they could vote, and you with your power of leadership, would direct their votes in the right channel, do you believe their condition would not be materially improved? I do, and you do.

Chesnutt had written Washington earlier, on June 27, 1903, and August 11, 1903:

I have no faith in the Southern people's sense of justice so far as the Negro rights are concerned. Their own public opinion on the subject is hopelessly corrupt, and they have poisoned the North until we scarcely feel that our rights are secure in this part of the country. The time is coming when every man who speaks upon these subjects will have to take sides one way or the other, and if you are going to stand with the Lyman Abbotts and men of that stamp, I fear you will be on the side which other colored men who have the interests of the race at heart will feel to be the wrong side. . . . I realize some of the difficulty and delicacy of your position, and yet . . . I do not see how the recognized leader and spokesman of a people whose rights are in jeopardy can afford to take a stand less high, or demand less for his people than white men do. . . .

I appreciate all you say and have written about education and property; but they are not everything. There is no good reason why we should not acquire them and exercise our constitutional rights at the same time, and acquire them all the more readily because of our equality of rights. I have no confidence in that friendship of whites which is to take the place of rights, and no expectation of justice at their hands unless it is founded on law.[39]

Even when the U.S. Supreme Court in effect nullified those rights, as in the *Plessy* v. *Ferguson* decision, Chesnutt did not give up. He held wisely that "there is still the court of public opinion to which we may appeal."

In an August 11, 1903, letter to Washington, Chesnutt mentioned another of his attempts to influence public opinion, "The Disfranchisement of the Negro."[40] In this well-reasoned exposition he points out the gains made by Afro-Americans during the years their right to vote was upheld as well as the subterfuges employed by Mississippi, Louisiana, Alabama, North Carolina, South Carolina, and Virginia to deny the franchise to 6 million Afro-Americans. He shows that, in effect, black men "in the United States have no political rights which the States are bound to respect" and that, thus unprotected, their condition has worsened in all sectors of American life.[41]

V *Premature Literary Retirement*

These trends and a revival of the doctrine of Manifest Destiny, the belief that the United States was destined to expand across the

North American continent and beyond, strengthened the tide of antiblack attitudes both in real life and in fiction which Chesnutt, other Afro-Americans, and a few whites of the time could not stem. The national conscience could not admit the validity of Chesnutt's position without acknowledging the speciousness of widespread systematic attempts, both legal and extralegal, to prove that black Americans were inferior beings in order to justify stripping these citizens of their constitutional rights. Convinced finally that under such conditions he could hardly cause any significant reversal of the negrophobic attitude of the majority of his white compatriots through the kind of fiction he was willing to produce, Chesnutt gave up writing as a vocation.

Ironically, at the very time he was relinquishing this first love of his life, Chesnutt received a highly satisfying indication of his reputation in the literary world: an invitation to attend Mark Twain's seventieth birthday party on December 5, 1905, at Delmonico's in New York City. Since only about one hundred fifty of the country's "most distinguished writers of imaginative literature" were so honored, Chesnutt did have the consolation of knowing he was recognized as an author by men who themselves practiced the art.[42] The generally high quality of Charles W. Chesnutt's published works, including anecdotes, tales and short stories, biography, speeches, articles, and novels, which will be analyzed in greater detail in the chapters that follow, supports the judgment of his peers.

CHAPTER 4

Milieu

Now, it is obvious that if one is going to draw a true picture of a life of a race or class of men, it is necessary to know the race or class or type thoroughly, its manner of living, of thinking, of feeling; its outlook upon life, its aspirations, its ambitions, its attitudes, its achievements—all the thousand and one things which go to make up its life.[1]

CHESNUTT'S choices of milieus for his fiction attest to his clarity of vision, his meticulous attention to detail, and his purposeful yet scrupulous selectivity of subject matter. His was a mind acutely aware both of the spatial elements and psychological aspects of his fictional settings, and of the realities of American life. He wrote mainly about conditions as he experienced or observed them during his lifetime; his literary ventures into the past are limited largely to events of the early nineteenth century about which he could have obtained firsthand accounts.

Although Chesnutt gave a number of locales cursory attention, he treated specifically and repeatedly the Cape Fear River area of North Carolina and metropolitan Cleveland, Ohio. Within these purviews he scrutinized what may be considered the most cataclysmic period in the history of the United States, from about the 1830s to the 1920s. Those years saw the American people shed blood in four wars for the twin ideals of freedom and democracy. Simultaneously there was a paradoxical subordination of those principles, insofar as many citizens were concerned, to the expediencies of rapid economic growth and territorial expansion.

The accuracy of Chesnutt's accounts of nineteenth-century southern culture places him among the best of the local-color writers. However, many of his works are more than regional in their scope and substance. When Chesnutt began to write seriously, during the 1880s, the literary trend in this country was veering from the Romantic toward the Realistic, in part because of the impetus of local color, or regionalism, which served as a bridge between the two modes. The influence of British writers such as Dickens, Scott, Hardy, and Eliot provided additional momentum for this regionalist impulse, which was strengthened as well by the many conditions in this country that Fred Lewis Pattee describes in *A History of American Literature Since 1870* as "the Second Discovery of America." With this geographic sectioning of the country for literary treatment came, inevitably, the necessity for both fidelity to milieu and careful portrayal of character. The South was especially popular as a milieu, and the Afro-American, a newcomer to the mainstream of American fiction, was a favorite though not a favored subject. Thus the trends of late nineteenth- and early twentieth-century fiction seem particularly appropriate for Chesnutt's artistic and social purposes.

One of Chesnutt's distinctions as an imaginative writer lies in his functional use of specific settings. He gave much attention to historically identifiable times, places, events, and individuals—all with appropriate natural phenomena, industry, architecture, folkways, and folk speech.

I   *Southern Towns*

North Carolina, especially the Cape Fear River area of his youth, clearly dominated Chesnutt's literary scene. Fayetteville becomes Patesville in *The Conjure Woman*, all the other Uncle Julius stories, and *The House Behind the Cedars*. It becomes Clarendon in *The Colonel's Dream*. Carthage and Wilmington retain their names in *The House Behind the Cedars*. Further, Chesnutt details the route, the distance, and the time in transit from Patesville to both Wilmington and Clarence (Florence, South Carolina) as carefully as Sir Walter Scott provides such geographical information in his Highlands romances.

Fayetteville is shown in greater specificity than any other locale. Under the fictitious names Chesnutt gives it, its gradual decline is traceable in the three works for which it serves as the main setting. In *The House Behind the Cedars*, set a few years after the Civil War, Patesville is a quaint old town which still wears the fresh battle scars of occasional fire-gutted buildings. Through John Warwick, returning home after a ten-year absence, the reader views these sights from various vantage points

and s\ e memories they arouse. The total effect is
remar\ a movie scenario. The market-house was

the cent\ Patesville, from both the commercial and the pic-
turesque\ ew. Standing four-square in the heart of the
town . . .\ r, with its four-faced clock, rose . . . majestically
and uncor\ . [It had once pealed] out the curfew bell, which at
nine o'clo\ ʰad clamorously warned all Negroes . . . abroad
after that ʰ\ ᵊenalty of imprisonment or whipping. . . . The
lower story \ ᵗt-house was open on all four of its sides to the
public square. ₍\ ᵤlding had] wide brick arches [and at] a certain
corner . . . steps leᵤ ᵗo the town hall above. On this stairway he had once
seen a manacled free Negro shot while being taken upstairs for examination under a criminal charge. . . .[2]

As Warwick continues his walk through the downtown section
of the old town "with which Time had dealt so tenderly" (p. 5),
he also sees a colored policeman (a change since Emancipation),
familiar churches, the old Jefferson House hotel, and Liberty
Point, still identifiable in Fayetteville, where slave auctions had
sometimes been held "in the good old days" (p. 8). Oates recalls it
only as the site where "39 patriots" signed the Liberty Point
Declaration of Independence on June 20, 1775, but R. C. W.
Perry, a descendent of free colored people in Fayetteville and a
relative of both the Chesnutt and the Perry families, was told by
his grandmother and others that slaves were sold there.[3]

Warwick's destination is the office of Judge Archibald Straight.
A Judge Robert Strange had resided in Fayetteville, but his office
was elsewhere. However, the office occupied by Mr. John D.
Eccles, "a highly distinguished lawyer and citizen," once stood
very near the site Chesnutt describes.[4] Across the creek
(Chesnutt's Beaver Creek) and easily viewed from the rear window of the fictional office were "the dilapidated stone foundations of the house where once had lived Flora Macdonald, the
Jacobite refugee, the most romantic character of North Carolina
history."[5]

Patesville has had a few more years to recover from the ravages
of war when it appears in the tales comprising *The Conjure
Woman*. The former Ohioan, John, who is the narrator of the
tales, is considering settling here with his wife. He notices that in
addition to the market-house

there were two or three hotels, a courthouse, a jail, stores, offices, and all the appurtenances of the county seat and a commercial emporium. . . . Patesville [was] one of the principal towns in North Carolina, and had a considerable trade in cotton and naval stores. . . .[6]

When "in 189-," less than a quarter of a century later, Col. Henry French in *The Colonel's Dream* returns to his birthplace, Clarendon, he finds it as it may have appeared to Chesnutt when he visited Fayetteville in 1901:

All so like and yet so different—shrunken somewhat, and faded. . . . The old town, whose ripeness was almost decay, whose quietness was scarcely distinguishable from lethargy, had been the home of his youth. . . . It was Saturday, and the little two-wheeled carts, drawn by a steer or a mule; the pigs sleeping in the shadow of the old wooden market-house; the lean and sallow pinelanders and listless Negroes dozing on the curbstone, were all objects of novel interest to [French's little son.].[7]

In sharp contrast, Wilmington as described in *The House Behind the Cedars* bustles with the activity which marks it as an Atlantic Ocean port, where great sailing ships from all over the world unload their exotic cargoes. The chief American commodities are, as in real life, "cotton and naval stores and products of the sea." The pervasive fishlike smell, the white sandy streets dazzling in the southern sun, and roads bedded with oyster shells are distinctive features of the lower town.

Although some of the citizens of Wellington (actually Wilmington) in *The Marrow of Tradition* accumulate considerable wealth, the "best people" cherish tradition, good taste, and comfortable living rather than ostentatious display. Symbolic are the imported centuries-old "carved marble fount" from which the Episcopal rector christens the Carteret baby, the tasteful furnishings of the Carteret parlor, and the broad acres of old Mr. Delamere's ancestral colonial plantation crowned by "a beautiful residence" comparable to "a baronial castle."

Patesville obviously lacks the vitality and the prosperity that characterize Wilmington/Wellington, but Chesnutt capitalizes on the natural beauty of the surroundings. A rich variety of flowers lends color to the weather-beaten Walden and Treadwell homes. The somber cedars and spreading magnolias in Mis' Molly's yard overshadow the brightness of some blossoms, but no comparative gloom is evident in later descriptions of luxuriant volunteer growth watered by shallow streams. Frank Fowler, journeying to Sampson County in hope of both selling his cooper wares and seeing Rena once more, comes to a place where

tall pines . . . overhung the road like the stately arch of a cathedral aisle, weaving a carpet for the earth with their brown spines and cones and soothing the ear with their ceaseless murmur. Frank stopped to water his mule at a point where the white, sandy road, widening as it went, sloped downward to a clear-running branch. On the right a bay-tree bending over the stream mingled the heavy odor of its flowers with the delicate perfume of a yellow jessamine vine that had overrun a clump of saplings on the left. From a neighboring tree a silver-throated mocking-bird poured out a flood of riotous melody. A group of minnows, startled by the splashing of the mule's feet, darted into the shadow of the thicket, their quick passage leaving the amber water filled with laughing light.[8]

II   *Northern City*

Cleveland, Ohio, as Groveland, is the only northern city which supplies the background in a significant number of Chesnutt's works. Its importance as a transportation center is emphasized both by its imposing "Union Depot" and the "fleet of ships that lined the coal and iron ore docks of the harbor"[9] along the Lake Erie boundary of the city. Its chief sources of wealth are lumbering and manufacturing, and the affluence of certain whites is evidenced by imposing residences set well back in "wide-spreading lawns, dotted with flower beds, flowers and statuary."[10]

III   *Regional Character*

Chesnutt patterns his characters after the inhabitants of the areas used for his settings. His imaginary southerners fall into the four classes of whites, the two of blacks (free and slave), and a group known as Croatan Indians.[11] Chesnutt describes the relative mobility among whites and stratification among the blacks both before and after the Civil War. The highest social class of whites (the planter aristocracy, prominent public officials, professional men, and business leaders) are represented by Judge Straight, Dr. Green, and George Tryon in *The House Behind the Cedars;* old Mr. Delamere, General Belmont, and Major Carteret in *The Marrow of Tradition;* and Colonel French in *The Colonel's Dream.* Examples of the rising middle class are

Lee Ellis and Captain McBane in *The Marrow of Tradition*, and William Fetters in *The Colonel's Dream*; and of the descending middle class is Judge Bullard in *The Colonel's Dream*. The third class of yeomen and mechanics is represented by Sheriff Wemyss in *The Marrow of Tradition*, white bricklayers in *The Colonel's Dream*, and nonslaveholding miller Dunkin Campbell in "Tom's Warm Welcome"; and the poor whites by overseer Nick Johnson in "Mars Jeems's Nightmare," the tubercular textile mill workers in *The Colonel's Dream*, and the slat-bonneted white woman who surreptitiously scoops up and eats clay in "Lonesome Ben."

Slaves themselves made distinctions among personal attendants, house "servants," artisans, and field hands. Chesnutt points out the animosity between the house "servants" and the field slaves in "Hot-Foot Hannibal," and in *The Marrow of Tradition* the snobbery of ex-body-servant Sandy Delamere, a black Methodist who considers himself as superior to the black Baptists as the white Episcopalians to the white Presbyterians. Slaves like Grandison in "The Passing of Grandison" echo, speciously, the contempt of their owners for free Negroes. This same scornful attitude is actually held by blacks of all classes for poor whites: according to Uncle Julius in "Mars Jeems's Nightmare," " 'in dem days any 'spectable pusson would ruther be a nigger dan a po' w'ite man.' "[12] Such whites, having little else, use color as their bulwark.

In stories dealing with the post-1865 period, Chesnutt depicts blacks in classes that parallel all but the upper class of whites, for actually American society was so structured that no Afro-American, regardless of his ability and means, had either the prestige or power in any community, North or South, equal to that of an established affluent white male. Significantly, John Warwick demonstrates in *The House Behind the Cedars* that a black man passing for white can achieve and maintain that status, thus implying that race prejudice is a major impediment to Afro-American progress. Mr. Ryder in "The Wife of His Youth," Mr. Cicero Clayton in "A Matter of Principle," and Dr. Miller in *The Marrow of Tradition* all represent the rising black middle class that, before Chesnutt, was virtually neglected in American fiction. The industrious father-and-son team of coopers, Peter and Frank Fowler, in *The House Behind the Cedars*; the fearless stevedore Josh Green in *The Marrow of Tradition*; and the enterprising blacksmith Ben Davis in "The Web of Circumstance" are from the bedrock third class (blue-collar workers), which at that time included a greater proportion of blacks. Shiftless Uncle Wellington in "Uncle Wellington's Wives," spineless Jerry Letlow in *The Marrow of Tradition*, and convict Sam Brown in *The Colonel's Dream* are among the "no-'count" Negroes in the lowest class of Afro-Americans.

IV *Speech Patterns*

Chesnutt likewise fashioned carefully the distinctive speech pattern of his characters according to race, class, region, and individual personality. Properly, he conveys no differences in the language of his educated, cultured people, such as Mr. Ryder and Mrs. Dixon in "The Wife of His Youth"; Miss Alice Clayton and Congressman Brown in "A Matter of Principle" (black); the Warwicks and Judge Straight in *The House Behind the Cedars* (white); Dr. and Mrs. Miller (black), Major and Mrs. Carteret, and the Delameres (white) in *The Marrow of Tradition;* and Colonel French, the Treadwells, and the Dudleys in *The Colonel's Dream.* In Chesnutt's view, although these individuals represent two ethnic groups, there is little if any difference in their speech.

On other levels the characters speak a dialect of some kind. The 1880s are referred to as the decade of dialect in the United States, for this substitution of " 'the real language of men' for the artificialities of genteel literary English" was assumed to lend still more fidelity to the regional writing then in vogue. But the presentation of dialect in print created difficulties if it was done too exactly. Chesnutt described his own treatment of such language as "the attempt to express, with such a degree of phonetic correctness as to suggest the sound, English pronounced as an ignorant old southern Negro would be supposed to speak it, and at the same time to preserve a sufficient approximation of the correct spelling to make it easy reading."[13] Thus he avoided the too literal rendering which flaws Joel Chandler Harris's southern Negro dialect. And unlike many of his contemporaries, Chesnutt did not employ "Americanisms or strange pronunciations with an eye solely to their potential humorous effect."[14] Rather, with characters on other levels as well as with Uncle Julius and other blacks and whites in his socioeconomic group Chesnutt made artistic use of speech to enhance both setting and characterization.

The words of wily Uncle Julius in the frame tales of *The Conjure Woman* are tinged with the indirection of the "bottom rail" (from "bottom rail on top," denoting a reversal of circumstances, and used especially in the South after the Civil War for the changed relation between former slaves and those who had owned them). In "The Goophered Grapevine," when Uncle Julius finds out that a northern couple are considering buying the vineyard which since the end of the "Wah" has been his private domain and which he wishes to continue to enjoy exclusively, he tells the husband, " 'Well, I dunno whe'r you b'lieves in cunj'in er not,—some er de w'ite folks don't, er says dey don't,—but de truf er de matter is dat dis yer old vimya'd is goophered.' "[15]

The sentences as a whole are fluent, echoing the rhythms and intonations of the speaking voice, and as befits persons with neither formal training nor cultural advantages, reflect various syntactical awkwardnesses; they are quite often a string of clauses joined very loosely. The slave Sandy in "Po' Sandy" provides an excellent example: " 'I'm gittin' monst'us ti'ed er dish yer gwine roun' so much. Here I is lent ter Mars Jeems dis mont', en I got ter do so-en-so; en ter Mars Archie de nex' mont', en I got ter do so-en-so; den I got ter go ter Miss Jinnie's; en hit's Sandy dis en Sandy dat, en Sandy yer en Sandy dere, tel it 'pears ter me I ain't got no home, ner no marster, ner no mistiss, ner no nuffin.' "[16]

Stevedore Josh Green's emphatic declaration of independence during the riot in *The Marrow of Tradition* differs from the complaint voiced by Sandy in sound, tone, and rhythm: " 'Now we're gwine out ter de cotton compress, an' git a lot er colored men tergether, an' ef de w'ite folks 'sturbs me, I should n't be s'prise ef der'd be a mix-up;—an' ef der is, me an' *one* w'ite man'll stan' befo' de jedgment th'one er God dis day; an' it won't be me w'at'll be 'feard er de jedgment. Come along, boys! Dese gentlemen may have somethin' ter live fer; but ez fer my pa't, I'd ruther be a dead nigger any day dan a live dog!' "[17] The Blue Veins of Patesville also use an obviously southern dialect. In *The House Behind the Cedars* Mis' Molly, who is illiterate, says "spile" and "min' " instead of "spoil" and "mind." Again, the imagery and vigor of folk speech as well as acute class consciousness are apparent in this canny assessment of the slick Jeff Wain to Frank Fowler by a countryman: " 'Yas, I knows 'im, an' don' know no good of 'im. One er dese yer biggity, braggin niggers—talks lack he own de whole county, an' ain't wuth no mo' d'n I is—jes' a big bladder wid a handful er shot rattlin' roun' in it.' "[18] All of these subtle shadings reflect Chesnutt's special attention to—and success with—the " 'stractin' " task of rendering a southern Negro dialect correctly.

He seems equally skilled in reproducing dialects of lower-class white people. The North Carolina sandhiller who narrates "Tom's Warm Welcome" recalls that when Tom crashed Jinnie Campbell's party

some o' the gals snickered, and one or two of the boys lafft out. But Tom wa'n't a bad lookin' feller, and was a good dancer; there was nothin' agin 'im, 'ceptin' his bein' pore and no 'count, so the gals wa'n't sorry to see 'im. An' as he would fight when he got his dander up, the boys was afeared to laff much. When the music started up ag'in, Tom mixed in with the crowd and got to talkin' an' dancin', and had almost forgot he wa'n't ax' to the dancin', when the old man Dunkin, who had'n' forgot it, come in to call 'em to supper.[19]

Again, the Irish cook and washerwoman who for a short time is married to Uncle Wellington in "Uncle Wellington's Wives" has a thick brogue:

Faith . . . an' it's mighty glad I am to see ye ag'in, Misther Payterson [Patterson]! An' how hev ye be'n, Misther Payterson, sence I see ye lahst? . . .
O yis, as well as a dacent woman could do wid a drunken baste about the place like the lahst coachman. O Misther Payterson, it would make yer heart bleed to see the way the spalpeen cut up a-Saturday![20]

V *Regional Diction*

While simultaneously reproducing natural speech patterns in authentic, intelligible dialects and differentiating among those who speak them, Chesnutt provided additional local color by putting regional words into the mouths of his characters. He was the first writer to use in literature the words "jim crow," identified as some kind of crude comb, and "goopher," an Afro-American folk term which is a synonym for conjuration. Chesnutt has also been cited for his use of *lighterd*, the South Atlantic dialect form of *lightwood*. Another folk term, *scuppernong* (the variety of grapes which Uncle Julius relishes), is of North Carolina Indian origin. Many North Carolinians have used *slat bonnet, piggin, ax, biggety, sometimey, passel, paddyroller* (patroler), and *A to izzard* so much that the words are categorized by specialists as parts of the folk speech of the Tar Heel State. All appear in Chesnutt's works. Other terms used by less educated North Carolinians, and in turn by Chesnutt, include *branch, creek, darky, cungeration, quarter(s), tacky, hillbilly, pass for, pin(e)ywood,* and *three sheets in the wind.*

Chesnutt also used a number of terms which were current in other states and utilized by several other authors in connection with their Negro characters on the lower socioeconomic levels. Harris joined Chesnutt in including *po' buckra* (poor white) and *paddyroller* (patroler) in the vocabulary of his Negro characters of unmixed blood. Page and Chesnutt alike used *juneseying* when referring to courting among slaves. Chesnutt, Harris, and Page frequently used *cyart* or *kyart* for cart.

VI *Folkways and Mores*

Unlike speech, superstition erases color lines, breaks down caste barriers, and penetrates all classes. During the nineteenth century North Carolinians—and indeed most of the South—as a whole had "a prevailing belief in signs, spells, spirits, and the supernatural."[21] Certainly superstitious beliefs flourished on the southern plantations, were clung to tenaciously by the Negroes and the poorer whites, and sometimes invaded the "great house." Chesnutt holds that most southern Negro interest in "conjuration," "hoodoo," and "voodoo" had become mingled and confused with the witchcraft and ghost lore of the white man, and the tricks and delusions of the Indian conjurer."[22]

Chesnutt's delineation of Aun' Peggy and Uncle Jube, the most powerful of his conjurers, includes their following procedures typically found all over the South. They exercised their powers in various ways, usually making or breaking spells. The most striking spell is transformation, which occurs in several of the Uncle Julius tales. In "Mars Jeems's Nightmare," Aun' Peggy turns the cruel plantation owner into a black man so that he will experience firsthand the agonies of enslavement. Mis' Molly Walden is certain that ghosts exist, having seen such a manifestation both of the infant son she lost and of its white father, to whom she refers guardedly—even in her thoughts—as "another she had loved." Both Mis' Molly and Rena believe in dreams.

Thus, after dreaming for three nights in succession that her mother is ill and needs her—and then getting a letter with the same message—the daughter goes immediately and directly to Patesville despite the obvious risk of linking her two racial identities. Old Mammy Jane, little Dodie Carteret's first nurse and a perfect example of the ex-slave black mammy in *The Marrow of Tradition*, is fearful that the small mole under his left ear marks him for bad luck. Moreover, she strongly suspects that Mrs. Janet Miller may have cast an evil eye on him or had as a witch sent a mockingbird as a familiar on the day Clara Carteret let baby Dodie almost spring through an open window. Mammy Jane secures good luck charms to protect him. When his mother finds one fastened to his crib, she does not remove it.

Chesnutt, like Mark Twain and Joel Chandler Harris, had unconsciously gleaned the basic elements of these and many other superstitions from the people around him during his youth. When in 1898 he submitted his "cunjah" stories to the *Atlantic Monthly*, he claimed originality for them, though he also thought them true "to the general 'doctrine' of conjuration."[23] During a subsequent visit to North Carolina, however, he realized that his real sources were the "dormant ideas, lodged in my childish mind by old Aunt This or old Uncle That."[24]

Chesnutt strove consciously to provide realistic settings for his works. Moreover, having himself become so steeped in the folkways and mores of the places where he had lived, he was sometimes unaware of the degree of accuracy he achieved in structuring the milieus for his fiction.

CHAPTER 5

Fictional Folk

"The proper study of mankind is man"; and, while a power of description . . . of . . . the beauties of nature . . . is a valuable possession for an author; yet the power to understand human nature, to depict the passions of the human heart,—its loves, its hates; its joys, its sorrows; its ambitions, its disappointments; its strivings after the infinite,—toward a higher life, and the inevitable opposition which it finds in [the] "house of clay," which binds it down to earth—this is a far more valuable accomplishment, and to master it requires a correspondingly larger amount of observation and study.[1]

CHESNUTT was aware of the significance of character in imaginative writing before he met the established authors and critics who offered him advice. In an undated statement of his literary theory, "The Writing of a Novel," he rated character as "perhaps the most important element in a work of creative imagination" and "good character [as the] highest product of the creative imagination. . . . There are characters in fiction which [*sic*] are more immortal than the names of those who wrote them."[2] Chesnutt evidently knew of no blacks so portrayed when he began reading critically. Accepting the Spingarn Medal in 1928, he recalled:

I observed, as soon as I was capable of intelligent observation, that the Negro in fiction had become standardized, and that there were very few kinds of Negroes. There was the bad Negro, as most of them were, who either broke the law or made himself obnoxious to the white people by demanding his rights or protesting against his wrongs; the good Negro who loved old "Massa" and preserved the same attitude toward his children as they had taken to him, that of a simple and childlike deference and respect—the good old Uncle and Mammy types; and the modern "white man's nigger," as we call him, who, as teacher or preacher or politician or whatever you will,

> "Crooks the pregnant hinges of the knee,
> Where thrift may follow fawning."

Then there was the wastrel type, who squandered his substance in riotous living, and the minstrel type, who tried to keep the white folks in a good humor by his capers and antics.[3]

During the time Chesnutt was concentrating on writing fiction (c. 1885–1905), prevailing scholarly and popular opinion of blacks was at an all-time low, influenced not only by social evolutionary theories but also by fundamentalist religious dogma. Belief was widespread that the Negro, whether created or evolved, was the most inferior of races; that even the possibility of his equality with whites was eons away; that God never intended the black to have equal power with the white man.[4] Despite the aridity and hostility of such a social climate, Chesnutt believed, as he declared later in his literary manifesto, "Post-Bellum—Pre-Harlem," that "a body of twelve million people, struggling upward slowly but surely from a lowly estate, must present all along the line of its advancement many situations full of dramatic interest, ranging from farce to tragedy, with many admirable types worthy of delineation."[5]

Though Chesnutt must have been more inclined to portray in his fiction strong, self-respecting, and aspiring Afro-Americans, as a realist he had to treat all types. His tendency to delineate more upper class whites, whether aristocrats or *nouveaux riches*, may be attributable to their prominence and power; a similar emphasis upon Afro-Americans of all classes is doubtlessly due to his greater concern for all of them and his deep-seated resentment both of their treatment in real life and their limited portrayal in American fiction. Moreover, as a "voluntary" Negro, Chesnutt devoted special attention to mulattoes "by depicting life as it is in certain aspects that no one has ever before attempted to adequately describe."[6] As a consequence his fiction had increased possibilities for novelty and drama.

In portraying slaves, Chesnutt only suggests the idyllic plantation life characteristic of Page, Harris, Allen, Edwards, Smith, Stuart, and Dunbar. He also reveals "the darker side of slavery—the old master's extravagance and overbearing haughtiness, the young gentleman's reckless dissipation . . . the hopeless degradation of the poorer whites, the slaves . . . bullied by overseer or frightened by the prospect of being transferred to the lower South."[7] Further, Chesnutt frequently makes such disclosures more dispassionately than does Cable or Tourgée. While disagreeing with Page and Dixon, who held that the Negro could not survive as a free agent in American society and that the freedman was the chief cause of Reconstruction ills, he remains completely realistic in showing that any ostensibly black man (Ben Davis in "The Web of Circumstance" and Dr. Miller in *The Marrow of Tradition*, for example) who has the same qualities and qualifications as his successful white counterpart cannot, because of obstruction by whites, realize the American Dream.

Unlike Tourgée, Chesnutt does not find that education will assure racial amity in community or personal relations. Further, he does not try to balance the social rejection of Negroes by whites, as depicted in Dixon's novels, by total personal interracial acceptance in his own writings. (Howells goes beyond Chesnutt to permit, in *An Imperative Duty*, intermarriage among the upper classes.) On the whole, Chesnutt's advocacy of the Afro-American cause seldom extends to the extreme of ideality of character or situation. He pictured people as he saw them in everyday affairs. By stripping away the façade of the stereotype, he reveals characters with universally recognizable flaws. In his delineations, many types previously serving only as vehicles of moral messages or of single qualities achieve the complexity which denotes human personality. Consequently, Chesnutt's black characters—regardless of their color, class, or economic condition—are clearly imbued with a humanity and worth conspicuously absent in depictions of Afro-Americans by most other writers of the age.

Chesnutt lets his fictional blacks express their own thoughts and feelings rather than reflect the attitudes of whites. Such treatment is very different from that of Thomas Nelson Page. Indeed, Chesnutt is so objective in his handling of white characters, even in racially mixed situations, that he was assumed to be a Caucasian until his racial identity was publicized in 1899.[8] But even after that revelation, most contemporary critics found his novels to be fair. While regretting that *The Marrow of Tradition* has "more justice than mercy in it," Howells admitted that Chesnutt does not "play the advocate . . . he does not paint the blacks all good, or the whites all bad. He paints them as slavery made them on both sides, and if in the very end he gives the victory to the blacks . . . it cannot be said that either his aesthetics or ethics are false."[9] In short, Chesnutt strove to treat all characters as "real, live, natural human [beings] and not [as] the creations of the books."[10] He recognized that elemental human drives and emotions know no lines of caste or color. His characters react as individuals to situations which they themselves create or into which they are thrust.

These situations reflect both the universals of human experience and special problems which bedeviled Americans, North and South, during Chesnutt's lifetime. Moreover, the perspective of the Afro-American character was unusual for that time.[11]

I   *Stereotypes Plus*

Instead of individualizing the mean planters and brutal over-seers who appear in the Uncle Julius tales and other fiction, Chesnutt stereotypes such characters; they are more important for providing insights into conditions to which the slaves had to adjust or avoid than they are as persons. Most of the wealthy plantation owners are strong-willed, self-serving, short-tempered, and sometimes dishonest. Their overseers ape them crudely. Colonel Pendleton in "Sis' Becky's Pickaninny" is obviously more interested in horseflesh than in human beings. He prefers to bet on and buy horses rather than prevent the separation of a slave family, two of whom he owns initially. Moreover, he does not have the courage to tell the young slave mother whose husband is now gone that she is being sold away from her child forever. Unfeeling Mars Jeems in "Mars Jeems's Nightmare" not only underfeeds and overworks his slaves but also denies them recreational activities after hours.

Chesnutt's capsulized description of Primus in "The Conjurer's Revenge," on the other hand, shows how unobtrusively the author transcends a stereotype in the case of the characterization of the happy-go-lucky slave, to create an individual to be reckoned with:

"Dis yer Primus wuz de livelies' han' on de place, alluz a-dancin', en drinkin', en runnin' roun', en singin', en pickin' de banjo [end of stereotype]; 'cep'n' once in a w'ile w'en he'd 'low he wa'nt treated right 'bout sump'n ernudder, he'd git so sulky en stubborn dat de w'ite folks could n' ha'dly do nuffin wid 'im.

"It wuz 'gin' de rules fer any er de han's ter go 'way fum de plantation at night; but Primus did n' min' de rules, en went w'en he felt lack it;en de w'ite folks purten' lack dey did n' know it, fer Primus was dange'ous w'en he got in dem stubborn spells, en dey'd ruther not fool wid 'im."[12]

Uncle Julius McAdoo, the actual spinner of the Uncle Julius tales, is an excellent example of a stereotype elaborated into an enriching, thought-provoking ambiguity. An illiterate former slave fieldhand who has lived on or near the McAdoo plantation all of his life, Uncle Julius seems as limited as his circumscribed life would suggest. He appears to hold himself in low esteem, as when in "The Goophered Grapevine" he offers to explain to John and Miss Annie how the scuppernong vines came to be conjured " 'ef you en young miss dere doan' min' lis'nin' ter a ole nigger run on a minute er two w'ile you er restin' ' " (*The Conjure Woman*, p. 12). According to John, the narrator, through whose eyes "the venerable looking man" is presented,

his curiously undeveloped nature was subject to moods which were almost childish in their variableness. . . . His way of looking at the past seemed very strange to us; his view of certain sides of life was essentially different from ours. . . . While he mentioned with a warm appreciation the acts of kindness which those in authority had shown to him and his people, he would speak of a cruel deed, not with the indignation of one accustomed to quick feeling and spontaneous expression, but with a furtive disapproval which suggested to us a doubt in his own mind as to whether he had a right to think or to feel, and presented to us the curious psychological spectacle of a mind enslaved long after the shackles had been struck off from the limbs of its possessor.[13]

Although, as in "The Conjurer's Revenge," Uncle Julius sharply rebukes a young black student for saying that the earth revolves around the sun when Uncle Julius "sees de yeath stan'in' still all de time," he believes strongly in signs, goophering, spells, and ghosts. Besides his apparent belief in all the marvelous events he recounts in the tales, in "The Gray Wolf's Ha'nt" Uncle Julius gets wet rather than risk having bad luck by coming up on his employers' porch with an umbrella up, and matter-of-factly attributes the balking of the horse in "Hot-Foot Hannibal" to the ability of gray horses to see ghosts on Friday afternoons. Again, he becomes almost an apologist for slavery at times. He declares in "Sis' Becky's Pickaninny" that he "had a good marster befo' de wah."[14] He also holds that "Mars Jeems" in "Mars Jeems's Nightmare" " 'wuz de marster, en had a right ter do ez he please'. . . .' "[15]

Uncle Julius obviously has some of the qualities of the stereotypic contented slave and superstitious Negro whose abysmal ignorance and inability to reason abstractly are taken for granted. However, these seeming limitations are otherwise belied, for Uncle Julius understands cause-and-effect relationships. In "A Deep Sleeper" he observes that he is not solely responsible for his inability to read. In "Mars Jeems's Nightmare" he suggests to his employers that many of the admitted shortcomings of the freedmen are traceable to their prior servitude; therefore whites, who have had advantages longer, should " 'make some 'lowance.' "[16] Similarly, by recounting "A Victim of Heredity," he convinces Miss Annie that since the conditions of slavery provided "some excuse" for the slaves to steal "chickens and other little things to eat,"[17] whites should be lenient about such thievery for a while. All those conditions and more are suggested in Uncle Julius's recollection in "Mars Jeems's Nightmare" that " 'dey wuz no use in libbin' at all ef you ha' ter lib roun' Mars Jeems.' "[18]

Uncle Julius also makes fleeting but unmistakable references to his better judgment and insight by observing in "Lonesome Ben" that " 'Mars Dugal' said dis yer clay wouldn' make good brick, but I knowed better' ";[19] and declaring in "A Deep Sleeper" that " 'Ole Miss wuz a mighty smart woman, but she didn' know ev'ything' " when she said, " 'One nigger man [should be] de same as ernudder . . .' " when a slave girl chose a husband.[20] He demonstrates a like ability to understand and meet the needs of whites by lending Miss Annie his rabbit foot in "Sis' Becky's Pickaninny," and by choosing to reveal the tragic outcome of a lovers' quarrel in "Hot-Foot Hannibal" shortly after Mabel and young Malcolm Murchison break their engagement. More often in the thirteen tales, Julius exercises his persuasive powers on John directly or indirectly through his wife for his own benefit.

This evidence that Uncle Julius, despite his disadvantaged position, repeatedly outmaneuvers John demands further assessment of the character. That the white employers can be so easily hoodwinked becomes more believable with the realization that they are newcomers to the South, a region which was then quite different from the rest of the country. Perhaps Patesville is Uncle Julius's briarpatch and he is operating like Uncle Remus's Br'er

Rabbit, a carry-over from African folklore which symbolized the ability of the weak to triumph over the powerful.[22] In such case John is not privy to all of Uncle Julius's thoughts and methods. John acknowledges their differences in point of view, but perhaps does not fully realize its import. In "The Goophered Grapevine" John, believing himself liberal in his attitude toward blacks, is unaware that his finding the shrewdness in Uncle Julius's eyes "not altogether African" is racist.

Uncle Julius, then, emerges as a clever character, wise in the ways of his world and of people anywhere, whose motherwit has enabled him to develop a means of coping in a hostile environment. He remains an intriguing enigma, an excellent subject for speculation, but forever beyond final explanation because Chesnutt provides no ultimate clues. Uncle Julius never divulges what he is thinking. The reader, whose perception is colored by his own experiences, must evaluate Julius solely on the basis of John's limited report and interpretation of his actions. In this respect the freedman provides an example of *Quashee*, a Jamaican term which describes a behavior pattern once attributed to the slaves, the most essential element of which is an "evasive, indefinable, somewhat disguised and ambiguous quality."[23]

Uncle Julius lends himself admirably to Chesnutt's planned first step in opening, through literature, the way for Afro-Americans to take their rightful place in the American culture. Here, in trying to make a positive introduction of blacks to the predominantly white reading public, Chesnutt offers a character of a familiar type, not offensive enough either to threaten whites or insult blacks. If a reader is only entertained by the tales, Chesnutt's social purpose, if not promoted, is not hindered. If, on the other hand, the reader looks beneath the surface, he will have to see slavery and its aftermath from a black perspective which at least makes a strong appeal to his sense of fair play.

In addition to stereotypes, Chesnutt depicts seeming stereotypes who turn out to be exceptional characters, and others who are uncommon in literature. Both because he knew that stories treating stereotypes were more likely to be published and that some people did fit those patterns, Chesnutt gave more attention to such characters, black and white, at the beginning of his writing career than he did after he gained some recognition as an author. However, many of his early characters who seem stereotypical are, in fact, more complex.

The most striking of the unstereotypical characters is freeborn Aun' Peggy. Slaveowner and slave alike seek and follow her advice to solve difficult problems. In "The Goophered Grapevine," Mars Dugal' pays Aun' Peggy handsomely in advance to goopher his grapevine so that the slaves will stop stealing the grapes. Moreover, in "Hot-Foot Hannibal" this same plantation owner fears even to upbraid Aun' Peggy for selling to Chloe and Jeff the doll with which they have conjured Hannibal, although the master has expressly forbidden such practices on his place. Admonishing Solomon in "Mars Jeems's Nightmare," Aun' Peggy not only demonstrates her power but declares herself " 'wusser'n de patteroles. . . . W'en you is foolin' wid a cunjuh 'oman lack me, you got ter min' yo' P's en Q's er dey'll be trouble sho' 'nuff.' "[24]

Chesnutt apparently found slavery so distasteful as an institution both to ex-slaves actually and to himself abstractly that he could not bring himself to feature a contented slave in his fiction. He states editorially in *The House Behind the Cedars* that "no Negro, save in books, ever refused freedom; many of them ran frightful risks to achieve it"(141). Grandison, a young adult slave owned by Kentucky Colonel Owens, is permitted to accompany his young master, indolent Dick Owens, to Boston because Colonel Owens thinks that Grandison will not try to run away. Feigning a Sambo attitude, Grandison has reassured the Colonel that

"I is better off, suh, dan dem low-down free niggers, suh! Ef anybody ax 'em who dey b'longs ter, dey has ter say nobody, er e'se lie erbout it. Anybody ax me who I b'long ter, I ain' got no 'casion ter be sham' ter tell 'em, no, suh, 'deed I ain', suh!"[25]

In turn, the Colonel contrasts Grandison's good life as a slave with living in Canada, where the woods are full of wild beasts, where the weather is frigid half the time, and the inhabitants equally inhospitable to "runaway niggers." Grandison, in the manner of a model slave, seems to be properly impressed. Dick, hopeful of winning his quixotic sweetheart by letting Grandison escape while away from home, provides many opportunities, but the slave forthrightly resists all temptation. Even after Dick, in desperation, has him kidnapped and held on the Canadian side of Niagara Falls, Grandison shows up at the Kentucky plantation a month later "ragged and travel-stained, bowed with weariness and upon his face a haggard look that told of hardship and privation." The reason for this exemplary behavior becomes apparent at the end of the story, when Grandison, his family, and his junesey (sweetheart) escape to Canada via the underground railroad.

Sandy Campbell (he and Uncle Julius are the only freedmen dignified by surnames), the body servant of old Mr. Delamere in *The Marrow of Tradition*, also has a multifaceted personality embracing the worshipful servant, man of integrity and pride, and the comic and superstitious Negro. Old Mr. Delamere describes him as "a gentleman in ebony." The extent of Sandy's devotion to the elder Delamere is shown by his decision to be lynched or sentenced to die for a robbery-murder the old man's grandson has committed rather than inflict the probably fatal pain of disclosure upon the ailing Delamere. In jail, Sandy tells "Mars John":

"Jes' one wo'd mo', . . . befo' you go! I know you're gwine ter do de bes' you kin fer me, an' I'm sorry I can't he'p you no mo' wid it; but ef dere should be any accident, er ef you *can't* git me out er here, don' bother yo' min' 'bout it no mo', suh, an' don' git yo'se'f ixcited, fer you know de doctuh says, suh, dat you can't stan' ixcitement; but jes' leave me in de han's er de Lawd, suh,—*He'll* look after me, here er·hereafter. . . . Fer I wuz raise' by a Delamere, suh, an' all de ole Delameres wuz gent'emen, en' deir principles spread ter de niggers 'round 'em, suh; an' ef I has ter die fer somethin' I did n' do,—I kin die, suh, like a gent'eman! But ez fer dat gol', suh, I ain' gwine ter say one wo'd mo' 'bout it ter nobody in dis worl'!" (208)

Sandy is not idealized throughout the novel, however. He has picked up some of his employer's Chesterfieldian elegance, but betrays lack of taste in his best clothes, an incongruous combination of an outmoded long blue coat with brass buttons and a stylish pair of bright plaid trousers. While his long association with the Delamere family gives him the strength to rebuke young Tom for calling him a darkey to his face, it also makes him snobbish enough to disdain the new generation of blacks. In the same manner he considers the Methodist Church, of which he is a pillar, better than the Baptist connection. Crushed by the disgrace of being turned out of church for having allegedly participated in a cakewalk and being too proud to confess a sin he has not committed, Sandy begins to seek solace in alcohol. On his unsteady way home one night, he is shocked into sobriety by the sight just ahead of a figure, dressed in his own Sunday clothes, which shortly thereafter enters the Delamere side door. Reacting to this seemingly incomprehensible situation, Sandy soliloquizes, "Ef dat's me gwine 'long in front, . . . den who is dis behin' here? Dere ain' but one er me, an' my ha'nt would n' leave my body 'tel I wuz dead. Ef dat's me in front, den I mus' be my own ha'nt; 'an' whichever one of us is de ha'nt, de yuther must be dead an' don' know it" (167).

On the other hand, Mammy Jane in *The Marrow of Tradition* and old Peter in *The Colonel's Dream* are mainly stereotypes of the worshipful servants who are also freed persons. They recall through the haze of years "the good old days" popularized by Thomas Nelson Page. (The accuracy of their recollection, however, becomes questionable upon the revelation that after Emancipation their former owners maintained no active interest in their well-being.) Peter, in the meantime, has suffered great hardship. Jerry Letlow, Mammy Jane's grandson and Major Carteret's office "boy," is a comic fawner who goes to any length to " 'stan' in wid de Angry-Saxon race.' "[26] Significantly, all three suffer sudden violent death because of their devotion to or dependency upon whites.

The most conditioned, genuinely Uncle Tomish of Chesnutt's characters is the diminutive Plato in *The House Behind the Cedars*, whose thoughts mirror his attitude:

Mars Geo'ge [Tryon] was white and rich, and could do anything. Plato was proud of the fact that he had once belonged to Mars Geo'ge. He could not conceive of any one so powerful as Mars Geo'ge, unless it might be God, of whom Plato had heard more or less, and even here the comparison might not be quite fair to Mars Geo'ge, for Mars Geo'ge was the younger of the two. (239)

Another youth in *The House Behind the Cedars* calls no man master, not even for money. Little Dodie Carteret's young brown-skin nurse, trained at Dr. Miller's hospital, is contemptuous of subservient Negroes; work for her is a matter of business. Finally, in *The Marrow of Tradition*, brawny stevedore Josh

Green beats almost to death a "dago" who calls him "a damn low-down nigger." When, while dressing his wounds, Dr. Miller suggests that he be more forgiving, Josh retorts in part:

". . . It 'pears ter me dat dis fergitfulniss an' fergivniss is mighty one-sided. De w'ite folks don' fergive nothin' de niggers does. . . . De niggers is be'n train' ter fergiveniss; an' fer fear dey might fergit how ter fergive, de w'ite folks gives 'em somethin' new ev'y now an' den, ter practice on. A w'ite man kin do w'at he wants ter a nigger, but de minute de nigger gits back at 'im, up goes de nigger, an' don' come down tell somebody cuts 'im down. If a nigger gits a' office, er de race 'pears ter be prosperin' too much, de w'ite folks up an' kills a few, so dat de res' kin keep on fergivin' an' bein' thankful dat dey're lef' alive." (113)

II *Great Emotional Involvement*

Despite the dehumanizing conditions suggested by Green's declaration, Chesnutt's Afro-American characters manage to retain their humanity. Though at the time blacks were popularly considered incapable of feeling deeply, these characters display all the emotions with the same intensity expressed by other races and classes of people. Blacks as well as whites evince physical and ethical heroism in the face of certain disaster; both are also base. Chesnutt describes the corrupting effects of power and privilege, and a corresponding absence of *noblesse oblige*.

A major example of heroism is that of Josh Green in *The Marrow of Tradition*. Ever since his early childhood, when he had seen his father lynched and his mother crazed by the attendant horror, the angry black giant had planned to wreak vengeance on the one member of the Ku Klux Klan mob whose mask fell off and revealed his identity. On the night of the riot Josh rallies a group of Afro-Americans to defend the Negro hospital. When it is set ablaze by whites, he leads the men out into a hail of bullets which do not stop him until he—preferring to " 'be a dead nigger any day dan a live dog!' "—smilingly buries his knife in Captain McBane's heart.[27]

Many of Chesnutt's characters, including Josh, are compelled by stronger emotional forces to take less spectacular but equally significant steps. Though Josh had been burning with the desire to avenge his father's death for many years, his actions were controlled by love for his mother. As her sole source of support, he has put off courting certain death by attacking McBane until after his mother has died. Tom Taylor, who since childhood has planned a similar fate for the murderer of his father in "The Doll," is likewise constrained to delay the doubly fatal slash because of his higher duty to live for his little girl.

Mis' Molly Walden in *The House Behind the Cedars*, Mrs. Harper in "Her Virginia Mammy," Mrs. Janet Miller in *The Marrow of Tradition*, Mrs. Cartwright in "The Kiss," and Miss Laura Treadwell in *The Colonel's Dream* are among other Chesnutt characters moved to sacrificial, sometimes ennobling, acts of love.

In *The House Behind the Cedars*, dark-brown Frank Fowler, the son of a freedman who is now an enterprising cooper, would gladly have given his life for Rena Walden. Like a chivalrous knight of the Middle Ages he loves and serves, hoping only to "win her friendship, and convince her of his humble devotion"(36). He had saved Rena from drowning when she was small; through the years he has performed chores and run errands cheerfully for her and Mis' Molly. After Rena joins John, Frank finds a job in the Clarence area so that he may worship Rena from afar without divulging her background. Later, alarmed by having his poor opinion of Wain confirmed, Frank drives his mule and "kyart" down to Sampson County to check on Rena's well-being. Consequently, under bizarre circumstances, he is able to fulfill his promise: " 'Ef you ever wanter come home, and can't git back no other way, jes' let *me* know, and I'll take my mule and my kyart an' fetch you back, ef it's from de een' er de worl' ' "(37).

Unfortunately, neither George Tryon nor Jeff Wain displays such nobility of character in his pursuit of Rena Walden. George Tryon reacts in an entirely different way after he becomes aware of his fiancée's ethnic identity. Initially he conducts himself as a kind aristocrat, becoming almost literally a knight in shining armor while seeking the favor of Rowena, whom he chooses as the Queen of Love and Beauty during the Clarence Social Club annual tournament. However, when shortly before their wedding he finds out accidentally what Rena thinks he already knows—that she is of mixed blood—his feelings vacillate from longing to loathing and back again. At times he attributes to Rena all the undesirable traits ever assigned to African and Afro-American women. At other times he considers trying to prove that she is white or, if this is impossible, of taking her away with him to live elsewhere. It is significant that he breaks the engagement and never again mentions marriage as a prerequisite for their living together. Later, when he finds that Rena is teaching in the vicinity of the Tryon estate, he proposes in a letter that they have a clandestine meeting at the same time he is half-heartedly courting a young white lady. Upon receiving Rena's unequivocal response that she wishes only to be let alone and forgotten, Tryon arranges to accost her on the road through the woods that she customarily takes on her way home from school. Her flight from him there fires him to follow her to Patesville, where her death terminates Tryon's harassment.

Mulatto Jeff Wain, toward whom Rena is never more than friendly, exposes his villainous nature by pursuing her too. He conceals his marital status when, as chairman of the school committee, he asks Rena to teach in his home community. Wain later reveals himself as so dishonest, domineering, and cruel that his wife has left him. Misled by his vanity into thinking that Rena's avoiding all his advances is coyness, he avails himself of every opportunity to be in her presence. Once, when he contrives for the two of them to be alone momentarily, he tries to embrace her, but is rejected. On the same day that Tryon has posted himself to surprise Rena, Wain approaches the same path through the woods with an identical intention. Like Tryon, he last sees the frantic Rena disappearing in the underbrush.

III   *The Powerful and the Vulnerable: The Black Male Dilemma*

As may have already been suggested by the outcomes of some of the narratives discussed, and as an examination of all of them confirms, Chesnutt's Afro-American characters, especially males, fare much worse than comparative white characters. The disparity is even more noticeable when blacks run afoul of any element of the white power structure. It can be argued that Tobe in "Tobe's Tribulations," Ben in "Lonesome Ben," Uncle Wellington in "Uncle Wellington's Wives," and Rufus Green in "The Partners" might never have been successful, even under ideal conditions, because of basic character defects. However, the same correlation between success or failure and dominant personality traits is not apparent in the fortunes of significant black and white characters who are contrasted in various Chesnutt stories. Black Dr. Miller and white Major Carteret in *The Marrow of*

Tradition are both highly reputable young professionals devoted to their families. Using money inherited from his ex-slave father, European-trained Miller has already built a hospital and founded a school of nursing for his fellow blacks. However, he attends all who seek his services, even returning to the home of the Carterets to save their baby's life after once having been refused admittance to consult with the specialist who had invited him on the case. The enterprising Carteret, whose wealthy aristocrat family had gradually become impoverished, found his ownership of the local newspaper profitable enough to invest his wife's patrimony in business ventures which he hoped would enable his son to take a place in the world commensurate with the dignity of his ancestors. Perhaps this desire, as well as Carteret's obvious race prejudice, facilitated his political alliance with the less scrupulous General Belmont and Captain McBane. Urged by them, he misuses his influence as a publisher-editor finally to precipitate "wholesale murder and arson" which he cannot control. Miller, though blameless, loses his little son, some of his friends, the hospital, and some community support. On the other hand, Carteret's family and future are as secure at the end of the novel as at the beginning. In "Walter Knox's Record" neophyte Knox (white) makes an error in judgment which he is able to rectify without great penalty. In "The Averted Strike" Walker (black) is able to keep his well-deserved promotion to foreman without a major disruption at the factory only because he rescues the owner's daughter and a friend from a fiery death. In "Dave's Neckliss," Dave is almost an ideal slave, and model freedman Ben Davis in "The Web of Circumstance" has built up a successful business and accumulated some property through honesty, industry, and thrift. But both, morally blameless, die young of unnatural causes. In *The Marrow of Tradition* young aristocrat Tom Delamere, having incurred gambling debts beyond his ability to pay, robs his old Aunt Polly and causes her death. He lives on, though less affluently.

Dr. Miller appraises the general situation very well in *The Marrow of Tradition:*

It was a veritable bed of Procrustes, this standard which the whites had set for the negroes. Those who grew above it must have their heads cut off, figuratively speaking,—must be forced back to the level assigned to their race; those who fell beneath the standard set had their necks

stretched, literally enough, as the ghastly record in the daily papers gave
conclusive evidence. (61)

Even white Colonel French in *The Colonel's Dream*, whose
motives are unquestionable, suffers for siding with blacks when
he thinks fair play demands it. After having been roundly
defeated by reactionary forces, he—unlike Dr. Miller—chooses
not to remain in the South. Even Miss Laura's appeal, " 'But, oh,
Henry, if all of those who love justice and practise humanity
should go away, what would become of us?' "(283) does not
change his mind.

That future looks bleak with men like General Belmont in *The
Marrow of Tradition* and William Fetters in *The Colonel's
Dream* amorally wielding financial and political power. After
twenty years of endeavor Fetters has more money than he knows
what to do with and reflects,

There had been a time when these old aristocrats could speak, and the
earth trembled, but that day was over. In this age money talked, and he
had known how to get money, and how to use it to get more. There were
a dozen civil suits pending against him in the court house there, and he
knew in advance that he should win them every one, without directly
paying any juryman a dollar. (225)

Marked by restraint, indirection, and elusiveness, William Fetters is outstanding as a character. Though this able opportunist
influences every community action in *The Colonel's Dream*, he
appears only in the last third of the novel, and then Colonel
French seeks him out. Fetters is so sure of his power and his influence is so pervasive that he remains in the background, quietly
manipulating the strings which control the movements of his
human puppets.

The most formidable of Chesnutt's villains, Fetters has the
anonymity of a twentieth-century crime-syndicate man. As the
forerunner of a certain type of unscrupulous politician or "God-
father" of our day, his evil is so monstrous that it does not need
the reinforcement of surface appearance to impress itself upon the
reader. Yet Fetters is not just a simple personification of vice, as
in the English morality plays, though the name *Fetters*—and
McBane and Letlow as well—indicates immediately the concept
of these characters which Chesnutt intends to convey.

The forcefulness of Fetters's character is also implicit in the imagery which Chesnutt uses as an additional descriptive device:

Clarendon was decaying. Fetters was the parasite which, by sending out its roots toward rich and poor alike, struck at both extremes of society, and was choking the life of the town like a rank and deadly vine.

Again, "he [Fetters] seemed to brood over the country round about like a great vampire bat, sucking the life-blood of the people." Referring particularly to Fetters's wanton destruction of natural resources while working the North Carolina pinelands for turpentine, Chesnutt wrote: "Like the plague of locusts, he had settled and devoured and then moved on, leaving a barren waste behind him"(118, 117, 216).

Whites as well as blacks were adversely affected by such men. In *The Marrow of Tradition* the power structure, represented by Carteret, Belmont, and McBane (the Unholy Three), cynically uses the masses to increase its political clout. The chilling potential of its influence is reflected also in the reaction of the blue-collar whites to slanted news items and editorials at the time the Delameres' servant Sandy is almost lynched for the robbery-murder of Mrs. Ochiltree and again when the riot occurs. In *The Colonel's Dream* William Fetters's convict-lease workers are white as well as black, although all his textile mill hands are white. When Colonel French visits the Excelsior Cotton Mills he sees the small unpainted company houses: "In the open doorways, through which the flies swarmed in and out, grown men, some old, some still in the prime of life, were lounging, pipe in mouth, while old women puttered about the yards. . . . Dirty babies were tumbling about the cabins." All the children from six years up and women through middle age were on their twelve-to-sixteen-hour shifts at the mills (113–115).

IV   *The Powerful and the Vulnerable: The Black Female Dilemma*

Even given their subordinate position as women in American society as a whole, Chesnutt's female Afro-American characters seem not to suffer defeat as often or as completely as their male counterparts. One reason is that they, more able psychologically than black men to acknowledge their vulnerability as the most potentially dangerous part of a minority group, react more often than they challenge outright. However, none of Chesnutt's black female characters meekly accept misfortune as their due. Further, they sometimes employ unorthodox tactics, both less risky and more likely to succeed than confrontation. In most cases, however, they persist; and if they do not prevail in situations of conflict, their adversaries pay dearly for victory.

'Liza Jane in "The Wife of His Youth," for example, is completely self-motivated and direct in her long search for her husband, Sam. On the other hand, Dasdy in "How Dasdy Came Through" uses a subterfuge requiring only a few moments to embarrass her rival publicly for the attention of the straying 'Dolphus. Though powerless, both the concubine Cicely in "The Sheriff's Children" and Viney in *The Colonel's Dream* remonstrate with their owners. For the extreme punishment meted out to their slaves, both men later suffer greatly, Malcolm Murchison for twenty-five years because Viney pretends to be unable to speak and therefore incapable of revealing the location of a large sum of money left for her former master-paramour.

The most consistently successful tactic is goophering or conjuration, as employed by slave Phillis and free Aun' Peggy. In "The Marked Tree" Phillis avenges the selling and subsequent killing of her son Isham by causing the death of the family and all kin of her owner, Marse Aleck Spencer. In almost all the Uncle Julius tales, Aun' Peggy safely "wuks her roots" to correct conditions, often caused by injustice, as manifested in "Sis' Becky's Pickaninny," "Mars Jeems's Nightmare," and "A Victim of Heredity."

V   *Mixed-Bloods and Their Progenitors*

Chesnutt's fictional mulatto children usually have white fathers and mothers with more or less Negro blood. Except in "Her Virginia Mammy," the fathers' negligence causes hardship for their dependents. The Anglo-Saxon begetter of John and Rena Walden in *The House Behind the Cedars* dies without making adequate provision for his children. As a result, John, unable to overcome the double handicap of racial identity and genteel poverty in his hometown, finds success elsewhere as a white man and unwittingly sets in motion the train of events which is climaxed by Rena's death. Although in *The Marrow of Tradition* Sam Merkell makes a will in which he reveals his secret marriage to his housekeeper, Julia Brown, and his fatherhood of Janet, who becomes Dr. Miller's wife, he never publicly acknowledges this family. Upon his death Mrs. Polly Ochiltree, sister of his first wife, suppresses the will and drives the mother and child from the home which is rightfully theirs.

The mothers, though less derelict in their duties, are not role models. Mis' Molly has many paradoxical qualities, whose sum evokes pity rather than admiration: continued allegiance to a dead white "protector" who made no provision for the contingency of his early demise; fading beauty; color prejudice derived from a white society which ignores her existence; great love for her children, which is in turn giving and demanding—especially of Rena; some degree of refinement; and illiteracy. The less aggressive Julia Merkell seems incapable of demanding and getting her just due. Unable to withstand Mrs. Ochiltree's continuing persecution and an unfortunate marriage, Julia succumbs during Janet's childhood.

Nevertheless, none of these and other mulatto children born of such mésalliances in Chesnutt's fiction is tragic or pathetic in the manner popularized by Cable. In a letter to him Chesnutt expressed distaste for fictional folk who are ashamed of their Negro blood and therefore lack proper self-esteem.[28] Such abasement is certainly not true of the now educated and prosperous Mrs. Janet Miller, who since childhood has hoped for some sign of recognition from her half sister, Mrs. Olivia Carteret, simply because they are kin. However, when extremity drives Olivia to acknowledge the relationship and even to disclose its legality, the black woman—having suffered too much in the meantime—rejects the overtures. Mulatto Tom, the sheriff's son, goes further by committing suicide after trying to kill his father, who belatedly wishes to help him.

Reacting in another way, John Walden in *The House Behind the Cedars* coldly reasons that if his ethnic identity is going to impede his progress, especially his desire to become an attorney, he will leave home and "pass." This is not difficult since he has "all the features of a white man." Walden is not ashamed of his mixed ancestry, but resents the barriers erected by race prejudice. Within a decade he has married well and become a successful lawyer and landowner. Nevertheless, he has been unable either to overcome loneliness for his own kind or to bridge the gulf, caused by his masquerade, between him and his closest white friends. During a surprise visit to his mother and sister, Warwick (as he is now known among his white associates) prevails upon Mis' Molly to let his sister Rena come to live with him. His love for the girl is obvious; moreover, his desire for her to have a better life must be overwhelming, for bringing her into his home greatly increases the danger of exposure which would result inevitably in disgrace, ostracism, and financial ruin for himself and his little son. Even after Tryon is privy to their secret, John tries to persuade Rena to come back to his household, to move with him and his little son Albert to the North or West, or at least to let him send her to school in the North. Though she refuses, he still holds himself responsible for her future and gives neighbor Frank Fowler a mule and cart in appreciation of his help during John's enforced absence.

John Walden/Warwick, who demands reader respect if not admiration, is shown almost exclusively in relationship with his mother and sister, particularly Rena, and with other characters who touch their lives. Rena, on the other hand, serves as the center of *The House Behind the Cedars*, interacting with all the main characters and evoking a positive response from all who come in contact with her. Emerging both as Chesnutt's most completely portrayed and most ideal character, Rena Walden/Rowena Warwick is unique in nineteenth-century American literature as a mulatto who "passes."[29] If she has a flaw, it is her seeming flawlessness by the standards of late nineteenth-century fiction. Even so, although her basic nature remains essentially unchanged, she grows in stature during a tragic round trip from a southern black middle-class society to a southern white upper-class society, a few hundred miles—yet worlds—apart.

Rena's physical beauty, in the classical Greek tradition, reflects her beauty of spirit. John Walden/Warwick, returning to Patesville after a ten-year absence, does not immediately recognize as his sister the "strikingly handsome" young woman with the "admirably proportioned" figure (the local white physician, Dr. Green, finds it "something on the Greek order"), "abundant hair, of a dark and glossy brown . . . plaited and coiled above an ivory column that rose straight from a pair of gently sloping shoulders. . . ." George Tryon considers Rowena, his fiancée, "the most beautiful white woman on earth," and his mother later discerns about Rena

> . . . an air of real refinement . . . not merely of a fine nature, but of contact with cultured people; a certain reserve of speech and manner quite inconsistent with Mrs. Tryon's experience of colored women . . . a fine, pure spirit, born out of place. (8, 102, 103, 217, 227)

At the outset Rena is typical of sheltered middle-class colored girls in the South around the turn of the century: docile, intelligent, morally upright, and naïve to a fault. Perhaps because of the circumstances which inclined the Waldens to live somewhat apart from their neighbors, the young woman is serious-minded and introspective rather than frivolous like Alice Clayton in "A Matter of Principle" or effervescent like Graciella Treadwell in *The Colonel's Dream*. Rena's love for "weak creatures . . . kittens and puppies . . . shiftless poor white, half-witted or hungry Negro" (59) is constant; moreover, her little nephew in Clarence and her pupils in Sampson County also thrive under her care and supervision.

In true southern style, Rena lacks her brother's avid interest in books and his daring initiative. Her ambition is to marry or to teach. She tells him once, "A man may make a new place for himself—a woman is born and bound to hers" (163). In the beginning she also easily defers to authority figures in her life, such as Mis' Molly, John, Tryon, and Wain, within the proper bounds of their respective relationships. She takes no active part in making the decision which takes her to South Carolina; she follows her brother's advice in not making a clean breast of their ethnic identity to Tryon; and, diffident about her abilities as a teacher, agrees to accept the position down in Sampson County only after Wain, as chairman of the school board, assures her of his active support.

Rena is as happy for her brother's sake as for her own that she wins complete acceptance in Clarence. Unlike John, she keeps in touch with her mother, rushing to her bedside immediately when she finds out about Mis' Molly's illness, despite the higher risk of disclosure now that she has promised to marry Tryon. Later, she similarly places the welfare of her pupils above her own, for instead of going home to avoid a nervous breakdown, she attempts to finish the school term.

Further, by the time Rowena and George become engaged, after a most proper courtship, she is so in love that she cannot envision life without him. Her total emotional involvement with this man is suggested by her collapse when he summarily spurns her, by her sleeping dreams of George as her beloved, by her fear of heartbreak or surrender should he treat her as of old, by her subsequent resolve never to marry, and by her indifference to a seemingly eligible suitor such as Jeff Wain. But a spirit like hers will not countenance bitterness, recrimination, or compromise.

For one thing, outright rejection by Tryon forces Rena to identify with black people and to become more understanding of their plight. Further, throughout her sojourn she has had grave doubts about the ethics of "passing." Recognizing the great need for Afro-American advancement, she decides to devote her life to the cause. Ultimately, however, Rena is alone. Just as her invisible blackness bars her from the whites, her manifest whiteness and air of good breeding set her apart from the blacks. Thus the temptation to fall back into the old ways—to walk in her mother's footsteps—must be great when George tries a different approach. However, disillusionment, with its accompanying pain, gives Rena a degree of self-awareness, personal esteem, and emotional independence which enables her to reject Tryon's improper overtures even if she cannot obliterate his image from her heart.

Rena Walden emerges from her trials in the black and white worlds as an admirable rather than an heroic figure. Because of her trusting nature and her sheltered life, she never becomes sophisticated enough to ward off male aggression. Nevertheless, she does not withdraw from life; once aware of her own vulnerability and man's culpability, she employs ethical tactics in losing battles while winning moral victories.

VI   *Other Woman Characters*

Rena Walden/Rowena Warwick overshadows all of Chesnutt's other female characters; their portrayal is either more limited or their characters less noble. Laura Treadwell and her niece Graciella in *The Colonel's Dream* deserve mention both as personalities and as symbols of the Old and the New South. Also in reduced circumstances, Miss Laura is unmatched in service to and sacrifice for her mother and niece. To supplement their meager income she gives music lessons to the daughter of the prosperous Negro barber, William Nichols. Nor has self-denial soured the gentility and sweetness which prompt Colonel French to declare, just before proposing, that verses from Proverbs 31 describe her:

Who can find a virtuous woman? For her price is far above rubies. The heart of her husband doth safely trust in her. She will do him good and not evil all the days of her life. Strength and honour are her clothing, and she shall rejoice in time to come.

French is convinced that she can meet all his needs and function effectively as his wife and Phil's mother anywhere. But Laura Treadwell, more realistic, knows that she cannot make the radical adjustment necessary, especially in her views on race relations. Neither she nor French countenances social acceptance, of course; except for the family who used to be Treadwell slaves, Laura has been so conditioned as to automatically place Negroes in a world apart in which they should be treated fairly. In deference to local mores and her personal inclinations, she avoids all but necessary association with them in a properly stratified relationship. Thus, when French asks her to accompany him to the Negro school, she cannot accept spontaneously—even to please him. Later, when French proposes to build a library for all the townspeople, she suggests gently that "the white people wouldn't wish to handle the same books" (163).

Laura's nearly seventeen-year-old niece is oblivious to such matters. A typically ingenuous, impulsive, self-centered teenager whose unruly brown hair suggests her spirit, Graciella loves faithful but impecunious Ben Dudley. However, she will not become engaged unless he can promise to take her to New York, the center of culture and excitement. Mistakenly believing that Colonel French is interested in marrying her, Graciella opportunistically breaks off with Ben. The basic fineness of her nature begins to manifest itself when she overhears French propose to her aunt. She is further chastened by rebuffs from young Dudley, but persists both in helping and becoming reconciled with him when he is in jail charged with shooting Barclay Fetters and seemingly less likely than ever to satisfy Graciella's desire to escape poverty and the South. That her emancipation on the race issue has also begun is evidenced in her immediate rejoinder, upon hearing that Uncle Peter's coffin has been removed from the

French cemetery plot that, " 'it was a shame! . . . Peter was a good old nigger, and it wouldn't have done anybody any harm to leave him there. I'd rather be buried beside old Peter than near any of the poor white trash that dug him up—so there!' " (285–86).

VII *Psychological Impact*

Chesnutt's characters speak for themselves—the blacks more eloquently than the whites as a whole, though it is evident that certain white characters are delineated better than some black ones. This difference is due in part to the author's identification with Afro-Americans, which gave him "an accuracy and insight not to be obtained by an outsider." He was also greatly concerned about the plight of Afro-Americans in life and in literature, and recognized the influence of one upon the other.

The manner in which he structured and presented his characters suggests that he was aware of the subtle and pervasive influence of the stereotype and would agree with Joseph Boskin in "Sambo: The National Jester in the Popular Culture," that "stereotypes are often so powerful that they can be dislodged only after a series of assaults on them."[30] The impact upon the American public (not just American readers) of derogatory stereotypes of Afro-Americans is incalculable. In 1890, for example, the Negro freedman was described as "one of the liveliest and strongest forces in our varicolored national caricature!"[31] He was exaggerated beyond recognition as a human being. Most often he became a comic animal. Since writing was his chief means of refuting such subtle psychological conditioning, Chesnutt sought through characterization not only to create viable images but also to show the fallaciousness of all existing stereotypes of Afro-Americans. At the same time he tried to improve the literary image of the blacks in the national mind, to show that circumstances rather than color are the major determinants of character, and to encourage people to see one another as individuals. He felt that he would make substantial progress toward his ultimate goal of a better way of life for all U.S. citizens if he could get the American public to realize that black and white alike are persons and that all are clothed in the frail garb of humanity.

CHAPTER 6

Themes and Issues

There is but one solution to the race problem in the United States, and that is to grant the Negro *equality*. I do not speak of something which is to be achieved. Men achieve liberty; they achieve civilization. The equality of which I speak is that of which, in the language of the Declaration of Independence, all men are created. It is the equality which is freely conceded between white man and white man. It is the right to share fairly and equitably in the use of the earth, which is our common mother, our common inheritance, our common grave. It is the right of the Negroes the world over because of their humanity. It is their right in this land if such a basis of right were needed, because of their nativity. Here they were born and their fathers for more generations than most of the white people who are trying to crowd them off the earth. And they are entitled to this simple elemental right by the Constitution of the United States.[1]

I *The Real-World Background*

JUST as the events in Chesnutt's fiction often parallel his real and vicarious experiences, so the themes of his imaginative writings and the subjects of his lectures and essays bespeak his major concerns. Chesnutt's lifetime saw the Black Codes and predatory violence immediately after the end of the Civil War; ratification of the Thirteenth, Fourteenth, and Fifteenth Amendments; the Civil Rights Act of 1875; the Compromise of 1877; the virtual nullification of the Act of 1875 by the Supreme Court decision on the Civil Rights Cases of 1883; widespread denial of voting privileges ending in almost complete disfranchisement of blacks in the South by the turn of the century (it was legalized in North Carolina in 1898); and general segregation and discrimination in all walks of life. Though these trends were less evident in the North, prejudice there against Afro-Americans was nevertheless widespread and sometimes laws safeguarding their rights were openly flaunted.[2] Moreover, on the national and international scenes the closing of the frontier, scientific discovery and invention, misinterpreted social Darwinism, industrial development, urbanization, increasing agrarian unrest, immigration, **widespread depression in the late 1800s and 1890s, and the annexation of the Philippines affected blacks as well as other segments of the population.**

The deterioration of the Negro's position is reflected in prevailing attitudes in popular literature between 1875 and 1930. The patronizing, paternalistic treatment of blacks in the fiction of writers like Joel Chandler Harris and Thomas Nelson Page was superseded by the venomous tirades of Thomas Dixon (born in the last year of the Civil War). The Afro-American was thus the actual and the literary scapegoat of white America.

These conditions and trends greatly influenced Chesnutt's choice of the humanity of blacks and man's inhumanity to man as his central themes. In a letter dated November 5, 1901, to Booker T. Washington, he expressed his commitment to "a literature of necessity":

The writings of Harris and Page and others of that ilk . . . have furnished my chief incentive to write something upon the other side of the very vital question. I know I am on the weaker side in point of popular sympathy, but I am on the stronger side in point of justice and morality, and if I can but command the skill and power to compel attention, I think I will win out in the long run, so far as I am personally concerned, and will help the cause, which is vastly more important.[3]

The astute Chesnutt realized that a substantial mitigation of the harmful effects, both spiritual and physical, upon both blacks and whites of their joint experience on the North American continent since the early seventeenth century was requisite for any meaningful change in race relations in the United States. The white majority were suffering from a moral malaise brought on by repeated repudiation of Christian and democratic principles in order to justify or condone the practice of legalized slavery. In turn, blacks, functioning primarily as the oppressed, were lacerated by the triple trauma of various forms of enslavement, curtailment of citizenship rights of those who remained free as slavery became institutionalized, and the constant, widespread derogation of all blacks regardless of their status.

For Chesnutt the doctrine of white supremacy (which he also labeled "the unjust spirit of caste") was the chief deterrent to public acceptance of the fact that as a whole blacks are neither inferior nor superior to other ethnic groups. He traced the attitude to differences in appearance (mainly color) and behavior as determined by the cultural backgrounds of African blacks and European whites, and reinforced by slavery.[4] Chesnutt also identified this belief as a major cause of conditions under which most white Americans and some black ones were unfair, sometimes to the point of cruelty, in their treatment of blacks. This state of affairs was quite evident during slavery and manifested itself thereafter on most levels of human activity throughout Chesnutt's lifetime.

II *The Humanity of Blacks*

For Chesnutt a successful treatment of the theme of the humanity of Afro-Americans required a replacement of an unfairly blemished image in the minds of blacks as well as of whites by a realistic one. He demonstrates that the Afro-Americans respond in like manner to the stimuli which, under similar conditions, motivate all other human beings. This might seem self-evident to twentieth-century readers, but even after the Civil War many people considered Negroes as subhuman and capable only of limited thought and gross emotions. They were portrayed in this manner by many writers of fiction, Thomas Nelson Page and Dixon particularly. Thus, by letting his Negro characters display basic motivating forces such as love, hate, jealousy, pride, ambition, integrity, and fear in lifelike situations, Chesnutt emphasizes their innate humanity. At the same time, though he portrays many characters narrowly, for obviously didactic purposes, Chesnutt conceals the utilitarian role of others under an appealing mix of personality traits which, in their lack of perfection, project the humanity of the characters and establish a sympathetic bond with the reader.

Of the characters already discussed in some detail, Uncle Julius McAdoo, Primus, the slave Dave, Aun' Peggy, Uncle Wellington, Grandison, Sandy Campbell, Josh Green, Mis' Molly Walden, and John and Rowena Walden/Warwick fall into the latter category. Frank Fowler and Dr. William Miller are almost too good to be true. Conversely, except for a contrived affability, Jeff Wain has no redeeming features. On the other hand, Chesnutt packs a maximum of appeal in his brief references to "little Mose," who inspired the title of "Sis' Becky's Pickaninny." This animated little fellow displays his affection for his mother by putting his arms around her neck and laughing and crowing when she talks with him. Moreover, when she does not come home from work as usual, not even Aun' Nancy's rocking can stop his crying until sleep overcomes him. Thereafter his eyes lose their brightness and he refuses to eat. Even "peaked," he wins both Aun' Nancy and her "old missis," who " ' 'lowed he wuz a lackly little nigger en wu'th raisin'. ' " In "The Limb of Satan" Chesnutt makes credibly amusing the reversal in the attitude of old Uncle Ebenezer P. Johnson toward the spoiled, mischievous, rock-throwing little Sammy Walker when he discovers that " 'dat little black lim' er Satan' " is his grandson. The same kind of indulgence is evoked by Dasdy's more questionable wrongdoing in ruining the finery of her rival and getting a husband in "How Dasdy Came Through."

Not only various kinds of love but also pride, fear, grief, jealousy, and revenge drive main characters, all slaves, in "Hot-Foot Hannibal," "Lonesome Ben," "The Gray Wolf's Ha'nt," and "The Marked Tree" to such tragic fates that the reader's empathy with the victims may blind him initially to the points of the tales. Moreover, contrary to a highly publicized myth, members of families or concerned friends make extraordinary efforts to keep the family unit intact and secure, as illustrated in "Sis' Becky's Pickaninny," "Po' Sandy," "Aunt Lucy's Search," and "The Doll."

III   *Man's Inhumanity to Man*

In turn, Chesnutt, reflecting the times, shows that neither nobility of character nor lack of it in Afro-Americans affected a white American's concept of them as inferior creatures, a belief which became deeply ingrained during more than 200 years of slavery. Indeed, he goes further to show that most whites always expect the worst from blacks, whether slave or free. Conditioned to have low opinions of Afro-Americans and mindful of the importance of keeping that minority in its place, those whites never give the blacks the benefit of the doubt. Thus, in "Dave's Neckliss," though slave Dave's honesty and integrity are unquestioned until he is accused of stealing a ham, his repeated protestations of innocence are summarily dismissed. Justice is equally blind in the case of freedman Ben Davis in "A Web of Circumstance." Disgrace and death are the undeserved fate of both men. Only the extraordinary intervention of old Mr. Delamere saves Sandy Campbell, innocent of the murder laid at his door, from being lynched in *The Marrow of Tradition*.

IV *The Doctrine of White Supremacy*

In *The House Behind the Cedars* Dr. Green expounds to George Tryon, in ringing tones, his belief in a racial superiority which permits these and other injustices to blacks:

"They may exalt our slaves over us temporarily, but they have not broken our spirit, and cannot take away our superiority of blood and breeding. In time we shall regain control. The Negro is an inferior creature; God has marked him with the badge of servitude, and has adjusted his intellect to a servile condition. We will not long submit to his domination. I give you a toast, sir: The Anglo-Saxon race: may it remain forever, as now, the head and front of creation, never yielding its rights, and ready always to die, if need be, in defense of its liberties!" (124)

Other characters, most of whom belong to the upper class, express similar sentiments in other fiction by Chesnutt. None is more rabid than the Rev. Dr. McKenzie in *The Colonel's Dream*, a former northerner who came South during the war, or more deliberately inflammatory than the Bourbon Major Carteret. Colonel French, who really strives to follow the Golden Rule, insists only that Negroes should have "at least *some* chance," because any mention of equality for blacks would arouse such hostility that he could not carry out his plans to benefit all the people in Clarendon. Even Jerry Letlow, the porter and general flunky at the office of the *Morning Chronicle* in *The Marrow of Tradition*, overhears so much about "White Supremacy" from the "Big Three" (Major Carteret, General Belmont, and Captain McBane) that he repeatedly mouths the malapropism, " 'No nigger damnation [domination]!' "

The rationalization upon which the doctrine of white supremacy is based essentially deny humanity to blacks and facilitate the sanction of injustices to them. Moreover, since this belief was so pervasive, all people within and between each race and all relations from the cradle to the grave were affected. Chesnutt shows some of the resultant conditions, ranging from verbal slights to sick violence, and often proposes solutions for the problems as he explores his other general theme of man's inhumanity to man.

Even though Jerry Letlow shrewdly perceives whites to be the wielders of power and therefore wishes to be white, and though—unable to effect this metamorphosis—he toadies to the "Big Three," Jerry resents not only being addressed pejoratively as "boy" and "charcoal" by McBane but also the latter's tossing him a coin to pay for drinks instead of handing it to him. Such boorish behavior might have been expected of McBane; earlier in the novel he had gone into the jim-crow coach, to which Dr. Miller had been banished, to smoke a cigar and then deliberately spat upon the floor as he left. Carteret shakes the hands of all his employees except Jerry when he passes out cigars to celebrate little Dodie's birth. Mrs. Carteret discharges her nursemaid when she discovers that the girl's sister works for "the Miller woman" (123). Moreover, Carteret will not permit Dr. Miller, usually addressed by whites as "Miller," to enter his front door—no Negro had ever darkened it—or even in the emergency created by Dodie's condition to let the physician treat Dodie in violation of the old southern custom of permitting only white doctors to attend white patients. To him all blacks are members of "an inferior and degraded race" (185). He even shares Colonel Belmont's revulsion at seeing two convicts, one black and one white, chained together and in the custody of a black policeman. These and other actions of the "Big Three" confirm the sincerity of their toast to " 'White Supremacy . . . everywhere . . . now and forever!' " (38–39). Finally, Ben Dudley in *The Colonel's Dream* becomes infuriated when Barclay Fetters mistakes him "for a nigger," calls him "boy," and orders him to open his carriage door or hold the horses when Fetters arrives at the Opera House for the Assembly Ball.

In his "The Courts and the Negro" (n.d.), Chesnutt relates that the judge in a South Carolina court reprimanded a white witness for using the title *Mister* in referring to an Afro-American witness named Jones, who was his employer. Chesnutt points up the inconsistency laconically: "The master was Jones, the servant was Mister."[5] In the same essay he also observed: "The growth of race prejudice, aside from any immediate question of personal advantage, but viewed merely in the light of class consciousness, is the most sinister feature of the whole race conflict in the United States. With caste firmly established, how can any man escape it?"[6] In an address delivered before the Medina Coterie, a club of well-to-do white women of Medina, Ohio, on or about March 25, 1913, Chesnutt recalled that once the eminent Afro-English composer Samuel Coleridge-Taylor was in Washington to conduct several concerts at which his "Hiawatha" was performed. His visit coincided with a "great convention of American musicians," which ignored him. Chesnutt conjectured that Coleridge-Taylor would have been lionized had he been white.[7] Chesnutt supplies a fanciful solution in "The Niagara Movement: Oberlin": "If the entire colored race of the United States could change its color overnight, there would be no race problem left."[8]

Of the problems which plagued blacks as a whole, Chesnutt gives proportionately more attention to miscegenation, mixed marriage, and the identity problems of offspring of such unions, including rejection by white relatives, "passing," and color prejudice. One almost extraneous episode in *The Colonel's Dream*, apparently a modification of "The Dumb Witness," treats miscegenation. Miscegenation and "passing" provide the major themes for *The House Behind the Cedars*, which Chesnutt himself said was inspired by the life of one of his relatives. These and similar themes, in combination with community concerns, account for the highly plotted *The Marrow of Tradition*. Six of the nine stories in *The Wife of His Youth* have such focuses, as do only incidentally "The Sway-Backed House," "The Fall of Adam," "Lonesome Ben," and "The Doll." Again, nearly half of Chesnutt's seventy-odd articles and speeches still extant touch upon these same issues.

In fiction and nonfiction alike, Chesnutt's stance on these problems is consistent. Especially in his narratives, Chesnutt eschews the romantic approach which would have permitted him to supply neat, ethical culminations in keeping with the sensible solutions offered in his essays, speeches, and letters. Instead he chooses to point out the conditions, especially those imposed upon individuals by society, which, in keeping with his times, prevent any such reasonable, happy resolutions. In short, he hoped that upon being confronted with their misdeeds, most people would be moved by their consciences or at least by a sense of fair play to rectify their shortcomings.

V *Miscegenation and Intermarriage*

In his Medina speech [1913], Chesnutt reiterated his belief that individuals should be free to marry whomever they choose as a right of contract. He pointed up the rarity of such unions, probably because of the general preference of individuals for partners of their own ethnic group and awareness that such a combination offered a better chance for a successful marriage. He also informed his audience that despite the greater personal and social difficulties faced by interracial couples, individuals still continue to mix. Chesnutt therefore condemned as legally wrong, morally pernicious, and personally insulting any laws forbidding intermarriage as were then in effect in all the southern and a few northern states. Moreover, such statutes relieved the white parties of rightful responsibilities for their actions and "put a direct premium on immorality. They deprive the victim of seduction of the only remedy which can partially reinstate her. It says to the seducer that he shall not obey the voice of conscience and seek to atone, as far as may be, for the wrong which he has done. It says to the innocent fruit of such a union, 'You must rest all your life under the stigma of illegitimacy.' "9

About 1922 Chesnutt noted that of a U.S. population of about 108 million, about one and one-half million of the approximately eleven million nonwhites could pass for white. Any movement to preserve racial purity, he continued, should have been started 300 years earlier by the white men who began the mixing and had had the power to terminate it effectively at any time during the intervening period.10 Years before, in the 1889 "An Inside View of the Negro Question," he had observed: "The much-dreaded 'miscegenation,' so freely condoned by a former generation of white people, when it was the result of unbridled license, and so loudly condemned by the present generation, when there is a possibility that it may some day receive the sanction of law, never was and never will be possible without the consent of the white people."11

Chesnutt's views on these issues are clearly reflected in the plot development of the fiction cited above. Accordingly, the major consequences of cohabitation of blacks and whites, before and after slavery, are dire. Only two interracial couples, Uncle Wellington and Mrs. Flannigan in "Uncle Wellington's Wives," and Sam Merkell and Julia Brown in *The Marrow of Tradition*, knowingly cross ethnic lines for their partners. In both cases the circumstances are unusual and the marriages shortlived. Their difficulties are traceable to personality flaws as well as to community mores which would have condemned the Bourbon Merkell for commiting "the unpardonable social sin" had he ever legally acknowledged his mulatto wife or daughter in life or in death. In "White Weeds" Professor Carson's negrophobia becomes fatal after his wife refuses to assure him that her blood is as white as her countenance; likewise, Chesnutt implies strongly that Clara Hohlfelder in "Her Virginia Mammy" would suffer emotional and mental distress if she knew her racial background.

Mis' Molly Walden is a prototype of the free mulatto woman who practices miscegenation, and her two children are good examples of the fruit of such a union. She "worshiped the ground upon which her [unmarried] lord walked";[12] only after his death and Emancipation does she begin to comprehend how much her acts of free will have compromised her and handicapped her family. None of the fathers, despite the good intentions of a few, makes any provision for the future of their nameless children; all the latter suffer grievously—with Tom in "The Sheriff's Children" and Rena in *The House Behind the Cedars* paying the ultimate price.

Chesnutt also shows that such offspring are often more hindered than helped by the circumstances of their birth. Except among their own kind, mulattoes occupy an anomalous position in their hometown communities. They are rejected outright by Euro-Americans—sometimes violently, as teen-age John Walden finds out when he insists he is white. John learns, too, that his ethnic identity automatically denies him study and career opportunities available to whites. Thus prompted to "pass"—a practice begun for similar reasons by many Afro-Americans before that time and still followed in the 1980s—John goes to South Carolina, where he can be legally white and practice law. He finds some support for this drastic step in Judge Strange's disclosure that legal definitions of race by states are as inconsistent as those made socially on the basis of appearance.

VI   *"Passing"*

Chesnutt himself found "passing" morally defensible "if it is only by becoming white that colored people and their children are to enjoy the rights and dignities of citizenship."[13] In "Crossing the Color Line" he gives guidelines for successful "passing," including very limited communication with black relatives, complete breaks with Afro-American friends, no discussion of race matters, and avoiding the limelight. In implicit recognition of the stringency of this step, he comments further that "the advantages on the other side are so enormous that they are coming more and more to be controlling."[14]

Chesnutt must have had these and similar conditions in mind when he both cautioned and demonstrated in *The House Behind the Cedars* that "going over to the other side" demands "sacrifice." Through John, who is able, and Rena, who is not, Chesnutt presents primarily pragmatic and essentially ethical reactions to the dilemmas of "passing." As a boy, John accepts the testimony of his eyes in determining his racial identity since he had been taught that God—who "made no mistakes—having made him white . . . must have meant him to be white," all earthly edicts to the contrary notwithstanding (145). Rena, on the other hand, never feels that she is white. Resentful of the arbitrary constriction of educational and employment opportunities, John feels no compunction about "passing." Rena is apparently contented to live and work within the narrow confines of Patesville's colored society; she goes to Clarence only at the insistence of her brother and with the acquiescence of her mother. John remains out of touch with his family for ten years; Rena corresponds with Mis' Molly at regular intervals and visits her indiscreetly. John, counseling silence about their family tree to Tryon, holds that George should accept them on face value; Rena must be assured that to her fiancé she is acceptable as a mulatto. To John their secret represents self-sacrifice; to Rena, sinfulness. Thus, when Tryon drops the Warwicks, John is saddened and embittered while Rena is shattered and shamed. He attributes the sorry outcome to human selfishness; she, to God's will. John plans to continue the masquerade, but Rena, anticipating the increased pressures to which he will be subjected, cannot go through it again: " '[N]ow I could never be sure. It [our secret] would be borne on every wind, for aught I knew, and every rustling leaf might whisper it' " (161).

Chesnutt recognized the moral ambiguity of some aspects of "passing" as presented in *The House Behind the Cedars* and anticipated as well the likelihood of its condemnation on both sides of the color line. Believing, however, that this evil had been spawned by another and having had an inside view of this social phenomenon, in the novel itself he makes an impassioned editorial plea to any blameless "dainty reader of this tale who scorns a lie" to put himself in "the place of Rena and her brother" before condemning their "passing" (116). On the other hand, under the circumstances as given, Chesnutt clearly shows race prejudice operating as an unnecessary, irrational, destructive force. John and Rowena are legally white in South Carolina; there is no discernible difference in their appearance and that of their white associates; they have demonstrated conclusively that they can live creditably in upper-class white society. As Tryon's wife, Rowena's background would hardly have been questioned—and never publicly. Moreover, after the fatal disclosure Rena is still the same person whom Tryon had seen as representing "in her adorable person and her pure heart the finest flower of the finest race that God had ever made—the supreme effort of creative power, than which there could be no finer" (90).

In this case, keen-honed white supremacy boomerangs upon its wielder after slashing the objects of its scorn. From the moment Tryon becomes aware that his Rowena and a certain "nigger" girl are one, he is torn between devotion to a person and disdain of a people. The mental and emotional turmoil he suffers thereafter is reflected in his fluctuating between anger and anguish, renunciation and reunion, throughout the remainder of the novel. In his hotel room as soon after his awful discovery as decorum permits, George finds himself unable to keep alive the indignation he had at first experienced. Tears flow unchecked at the thought of his irretrievable loss. Conflicting emotions swing in his consciousness like the pendulum of the markethouse clock that tolls the tortured hours. When Tryon finally sleeps fitfully, he has for the first time the recurring nightmare in which Rowena, standing before him, changes from a beautiful young white woman to a hideous black hag. Later, unable either to find happiness without his former fiancée or to overcome his race prejudice, George seeks to establish a questionable relationship with Rena, which she rejects.[15] Her death precludes any resolution of the dilemma, but Tryon's actions indicate that he will never again know the bliss he found in his first love. This senseless waste of life and happiness is another American tragedy.

VII *Color Prejudice*

On a lesser scale, Chesnutt also attacks color prejudice, another harmful social phenomenon. For example, he chastised "Blue

Vein Society" groups good-naturedly for their color bias—but approved their coming together to share common interests, causes, and aspirations. However, he also observed and made literary capital of the fine irony of the adherence of some of them to the same values which kept them outside the pale of white society and divided within their own.

Mis' Molly Walden in *The House Behind the Cedars* (surprisingly like old Mrs. Treadwell in her reluctance to accept the realities of post–Civil War life) and Cicero "Brotherhood" Clayton in "A Matter of Principle" both have strong feelings about color which diminish their character. Mis' Molly's life experiences have been so limited that she cannot see that her patronizing of the enterprising Fowlers, especially Frank, borders on the ridiculous. Peter Fowler and his wife are understandably resentful of being called upon when help is needed but never considered as equals. Mis' Molly decides against Frank's being invited to Mary B.'s party for Jeff Wain at the Walden home for fear all the other guests, mostly "bright mulattoes," will slight him because of his darker color. Her notion of a satisfactory compromise is for Frank to enjoy the festivities from the vantage point of the back porch. His continued magnanimity in the face of such effrontery exasperates his father and further diminishes Mis' Molly while enhancing the young man. Further, the pretensions of this group become laughable when juxtaposed against the refinement of the Clarence, S.C., circle of which Rena so recently had been a part.

Clayton, who should have known better if only because of his contacts with all colors of people in the process of becoming a successful businessman in Groveland, humiliates his family because of his narrowness. Although he is constantly calling for "a clearer conception of the brotherhood of man," he declines "to associate to any considerable extent with black people" and has indoctrinated his daughter Alice to believe that whiter is better.[16] Thus, when he is led to believe that a "palpably, aggressively black" man is the visiting congressman—who actually meets the family's standards for a son-in-law—Clayton's inhospitable actions cause Alice to lose her best prospect for a husband to a rival Blue-Vein belle.[17]

On the other hand, for some of these Blue Veins, as with Chesnutt the man, character transcends color and culture. Mr. Ryder in "The Wife of His Youth" is an outstanding example.

Now past middle age, and having improved himself to the point of becoming the Dean of the Groveland Blue Veins, he is about to propose to Mrs. Molly Dixon, a young widowed school teacher both fairer in complexion and more educated than he. On the day of the ball he is giving as the occasion for his proposal, he encounters a toothless little old black woman who, he realizes with a shock, is the former slave wife to whom he is no longer legally obligated. Nevertheless, Mr. Ryder acknowledges her before the guests assembled that evening instead of announcing his engagement as hoped; all those present approve. Likewise, Uncle Solomon Grundy in "The Sway-Backed House" follows the dictates of his better nature in remembering his "very dark" relatives in his will despite his oft-repeated aversion to them. The high moral import here is clear.

These examples illustrate Chesnutt's position that color should be discounted in any judgment of individuals. He presented such views forcefully in "Race Prejudice; Its Causes and Its Cure," in *Alexander's Magazine*, July 1905:

Why should a man be proud any more than he should be ashamed of a thing for which he is not at all responsible? Manly self-respect, based upon one's humanity, a self-respect which claims nothing for color and yields nothing to color, every man should cherish. But the Negro in the United States has suffered too much from the race pride of other people to justify him in cultivating something equally offensive for himself.[18]

Color, most often meaning race, was to Chesnutt the chief deterrent to blacks becoming first-class citizens in the United States. He said again and again that the surest solution to the race problem was disappearance of the difference in color, that is, race-mixing. Then, he reasoned, race prejudice would have nothing upon which to thrive. However, he always hastened to add that such a change, if it ever took place and was permitted to proceed naturally, would be gradual and not likely to occur for at least five hundred years. In the meantime he proposed that "all of us, white and Colored [*sic*], . . . resolutely shut our eyes to those differences and [learn] to judge men by other standards."[19]

Chesnutt made what is perhaps his ultimate statement on the race problem in a letter of November [?], 1904, to Booker T. Washington: "Anything I might say on the race problem would simply amount to this: that I do not accept for myself (nor would I ask anyone to accept) as a final solution of it, anything less than the principle which recognizes the equality of all men before the law and extends to every man an equal opportunity in all human activity."[20] More specifically, he told a predominantly black Washington, D.C., audience on October 6, 1908, that "the Negro is not entitled to any more rights than are other men . . . [but] the Negro is entitled to all the rights that other men are."[21]

VIII *Rights*

Chesnutt identified two broad categories of these rights: the private or social and the public. Under the first an individual would "be supreme within the walls of his own house" and "select his own associates" without imposed restrictions. In the public sphere, one would be free to participate, on the same basis as other citizens, in all the activities which as a whole constitute the fabric of our society as well as to use in the same manner the services provided for the general public.[22]

Chesnutt, ever the realist—perhaps a bit of a cynic—saw the American people as "a race of climbers," but not, as he explained, in a disparaging way. When, in his opinion, a white person considers a black his equal in other respects and "feels that it will be of value to him, financially, intellectually or socially, to court [that black's] acquaintance, he will go after it like he does after everything else he wants."[23] It was obvious that securing the rights of Afro-Americans in the public sphere would implement if not facilitate the successful storming of the "last citadel," social discrimination, in the fight for equality. Thus Chesnutt strove vigorously for the enactment or repeal of laws and the changing of public opinion and custom on all matters of segregation and discrimination in the public sphere. If by this means the legal and extralegal barriers to the social advancement of blacks could be removed, he was willing "to leave to time and to the operation of natural laws . . . [their] reception into private society. . . ."[24]

IX *Voting*

Chesnutt, as might be expected of one with his legal background and occupation, considered the ballot the Afro-American's best single means of getting and maintaining his rights in the United States. On this issue, as has already been indicated, he debated privately for years with Booker T. Washington, the most influential black man of his generation. Chesnutt seemed more alarmed than Washington that proposed restrictions on voting, some of which seemed reasonable, would be applied unfairly to deprive blacks of the franchise and that white southern sentiment would justify any means to keep the ballot out of Afro-American hands. His worst fears were confirmed in statements made by influential leaders as well as by passage of state disfranchisment amendments.

Though Chesnutt appreciated Washington's dependence upon local white goodwill and white philanthropy nationwide for the development of Tuskegee Institute, he nevertheless did "not see how the recognized leader and spokesman of a people whose rights are in jeopardy can afford to take a stand less high, or demand less for his people than white men do. . . . I want my rights and all of them, and I ask no more for myself than I would demand for every Negro in the South. If the white South will continue to ignore the Constitution and violate the laws, it must be with no consent of mine, and with no word that can be twisted into the approval or condonation of their unjust and unlawful course."[25] In a letter to Washington dated November 3, 1906, Chesnutt quoted from a pamphlet by "Mr. Fleming," a white, who condemned the proposed disfranchisement of blacks in Georgia: "Surely in a country where every one [*sic*] else votes and the suffrage is freely conceded to foreigners in a great many States, including I believe Alabama, as soon as they declare their intention to become citizens, it is not only a great lapse from the ideal, but the rankest sort of injustice that any different rule should be applied to so numerous and important a class of the population as the Negro constitutes in the South. . . . The practical difficulties I admit are enormous, but the value of equal citizenship is so great and so vital that it is worth whatever it may cost. Slavery was as deeply entrenched as race prejudice, yet it fell. And the sound of the trumpets[,] you will remember[,] shook down the walls of Jericho."[26]

Chesnutt also showed independence of thought in a short 1915 essay on woman suffrage for an Afro-American publication. He held that, since the broadening of woman's sphere beyond the family and home differentiates women from men as a class, neither their rights nor their safeguards against oppression can "be left with entire safety solely in the hands of men . . . and the ballot is the most effective weapon by which these things can be accomplished."[27]

Both because of his deep convictions and because the turn of the century was marked by increasing legal disfranchisement of his people, Chesnutt also criticized on the podium and in the press Washington's more moderate position on voting.[28]

Washington concurred with Chesnutt that "the ballot is valuable and should not be surrendered," but held "that we have got to depend in the main for our final rights upon local public sentiment and upon our increase in possession of knowledge and wealth and character."[29] In one short story, "The Web of Circumstance," Chesnutt shows the precariousness of such a position. In that narrative Ben Davis, a successful ex-slave blacksmith in a North Carolina town, has all the attributes—or their equivalents—that Washington cites for Negro advancement: a trade, property, and an unblemished reputation for industry and honesty. Yet he is as much a victim of an all-white criminal justice system controlled by elected and appointed officials, a politically ambitious state's attorney, a prejudiced defense attorney, and indifferent and insecure white acquaintances as he is of the covetousness of his helper and the infidelity of his wife. Although he has boasted to her that " 'dere ain' nothing like propputy ter make a pusson feel like a man,' " he is shown to have no means of avoiding five years at hard labor and subsequent ruin after having been framed for the theft of a buggy whip he had admired.[30]

X *Politics*

In both *The Marrow of Tradition* and *The Colonel's Dream* Chesnutt shows the great value of political power—secured and held through the ballot—and the great lengths to which some whites will go to get and keep it. The "Big Three" (Belmont, Carteret, and McBane) in *The Marrow of Tradition* and Fetters in *The Colonel's Dream* are among those "venal and self-seeking politicians, bent upon regaining their own ascendancy at any cost" to the detriment of blacks and whites alike.[31] Each having an "axe to grind," the trio has come together on the common ground of "White Supremacy" to secure wealth and power. Fetters, on the other hand, has enough of both to need no confederates and is too amoral to delude himself about his motives.

The misuse of political power often results in conditions, not always traceable to the actual power brokers, which Chesnutt constantly criticizes. As shown in the novels, many of the victims, unaware that they are being manipulated, often contribute to their own embarrassment or misfortune.

Through yellow journalism tactics in Carteret's *Morning Chronicle* as well as "by fraud . . . terrorism . . . and . . . the resistless moral force of the united whites," the "notorious 'grand-father clause' " is amended to the North Carolina Constitution(240). However, not content to wait the two years required for this total disfranchisement of Afro-Americans to become effective, the conspirators decide two months before a local election to make the Negroes afraid to vote. Under this cover they plan also to drive out of town, in addition to all the white Republican officeholders, certain blacks who are too outspoken or whose money-making enterprises can be taken over profitably by whites. Those excepted are significant: the collector of the port, to avoid trouble with the federal government; the "nigger preachers," who can be forced to endorse the takeover; and "Miller"—over McBane's objection to him as a "smart nigger"—because "without a constituency [he] will no longer be an object of fear." Using the old *Afro-American Banner* editorial as an incendiary, Carteret fires up a mob. When "the baser element of the white population" takes over, the mob gets out of hand and causes extensive loss of life and property. The novel concludes on this climactic day.

Other similarities—if not parallels—are also apparent in both *The Marrow of Tradition* and *The Colonel's Dream*. In *The Marrow of Tradition* Major Carteret is dissatisfied with public affairs in Wellington (Wilmington) because "at the last state election his own party, after an almost unbroken rule of twenty years, had been defeated by the so-called 'Fusion' ticket"(30).

The "Big Three," who have their real counterparts in the "early campaign committee of twenty business men" and the later Democratic " 'Secret Nine' " of Wilmington, are aided and abetted by the unnamed governor from a neighboring state, clearly inspired by one-eyed Ben Tillman of South Carolina (his ocular disability is suffered permanently by McBane in *The Marrow of Tradition* and temporarily by Barclay Fetters in *The Colonel's Dream*). Their joint efforts successfully culminate in the riot ostensibly caused by Barber's *Banner* editorial. This article is much the same as the one by editor Alex L. Manly in the Wilmington *Daily Record*, a Negro paper. Chesnutt's version of the cause of the fictional riot and Mabry's account of one resolution passed by the Democratic meeting in Wilmington on November 9, 1898, are almost identical: whites will " 'no longer be ruled . . . by men of African origin,' " and they intend to put the interests of the white race first in politics and economics. Likewise, Chesnutt's version of the political tug of war to ratify the Grandfather Clause follows historical accounts. His only substantial omission is the intimidating Red Shirt parade which took place in Wilmington early in the autumn of 1898.

No such violence or confrontation occurs in *The Colonel's Dream*, which is in many ways a sequel to *The Marrow of Tradition*. In Clarendon blacks have lost ground. They are a numerical minority, no Negro has "held a state office for twenty years," none serves on juries, "and when a Negro met a white man, he gave him the wall, even if it were necessary to take the gutter to do so" (193). Nevertheless, a candidate for governor, introduced at a meeting by the editor of the Clarendon *Anglo-Saxon*, flogs the dead horse of Negro domination and ends his diatribe with, " 'Equality anywhere, means ultimately, equality everywhere. Equality at the polls means social equality; social equality means intermarriage and corruption of blood, and degeneration and decay. What gentleman here would want his daughter to marry a blubber-lipped, cocoanut-headed, kidney-footed, etc., etc., nigger?' " (194).

Under such conditions none of Chesnutt's fictional characters attempts to pursue a political career. His aim rather is to show how they were being deprived of their voting rights unfairly and unnecessarily, as official records and revisionist history seem to confirm.

French, in *The Colonel's Dream*, like Cable, Tourgée, Atticus Haygood, John Spencer Bassett, and Judge Thomas G. Jones in real life, is the most vocal of a small minority of whites who believe in fairer treatment of blacks. Before being silenced by the reactionaries, he tries to explain during friendly discussions that

the best interests of the State lay in uplifting every element of the people . . . that the white race could hold its own, with the Negroes or against them, in any conceivable state of political equality . . . and that any restriction of rights that rested upon anything but impartial justice, was bound to re-act, as slavery had done, upon the prosperity and progress of the State. (194–95)

Because of Chesnutt's constant agitation of "one of the most important phases of the [Negro] problem," he was invited by James Pott & Co. to contribute an essay, "The Disfranchisement of the Negro," to "a volume presenting the Negro problem from the Negro's point of view." In it Chesnutt points out the constitutional basis of the Afro-American's right to vote; the progress blacks made while exercising the ballot; a description of the restrictions then in effect in Mississippi, Louisiana, Alabama, North Carolina, South Carolina, and Virginia; the ineffectiveness of Supreme Court rulings on these restrictions; the consequent denial of Negro representation in any governmental body; and the resulting disabilities in every sector of American life.[32] Chesnutt declared that the direct remedy for the disfranchisement of the Negro was political action. He also recommended appeal to the public conscience.

XI   *The Civil and Criminal Justice Systems*

Chesnutt's writings also treat the shortcomings of the civil and criminal justice systems. Three of his early short pieces, "A Cause Célèbre," "A Soulless Corporation," and "A Busy Day in a Lawyer's Office," satirize the flaws of would-be claimants and courtroom habitués as he must have observed them from day to day as a court stenographer. Later stories, more serious in tone, show how unfairly blacks and poor whites are treated. Ben Davis in "A Web of Circumstance" cannot even testify on his own behalf. Judge Hart is obviously prejudiced: he sentences Ben to five years at hard labor for the alleged theft of a whip, but gives one young white man only one year in the penitentiary for manslaughter and another just six months in the county jail plus a $100 fine and court costs for forgery. These officials and most of the men in the Clarendon community who might be called for jury duty are so indebted to Bill Fetters that they always tip the scales of justice in his favor. In *The Marrow of Tradition* the sheriff " 'has a white face and a whiter liver. He does not dare call out the militia to protect' " Sandy Campbell when he is in danger of being lynched and Judge Everton refuses to " 'move in the matter' " (191, 193). Similarly, in *The Colonel's Dream* the sheriff does not resist the mob that takes Bud Johnson from jail and lynches him. Moreover, "the coroner's jury returned a verdict of suicide, a grim joke which evoked some laughter" (278). In "The Sheriff's Children," Sheriff Campbell, who protects the life of his prisoner Tom with his own, is clearly exceptional.

XII   Convict Lease

Old Mr. Delamere in *The Marrow of Tradition* deplores the kind of breakdown in the administration of justice which in *The Colonel's Dream* the Negro schoolteacher Henry Taylor details to Colonel French as the main reason why his people do not always cooperate with enforcers of the law. French, in seeking to buy back Bud Johnson's time from Bill Fetters under the state convict-lease system, is thwarted not only by Fetters's corrupt connections up to the national level but also by local condonation of convict leases. Appleton, editor of the *Anglo-Saxon*, rationalizes:

We have so many idle, ignorant Negroes that something must be done to make them work, or else they'll steal, and to keep them in their place, or they would run over us . . . niggers don't look at imprisonment and enforced labour in the same way white people do—they are not conscious of any disgrace attending stripes or the ball and chain. The State is poor; our white children are suffering for lack of education, and yet we have to spend a large amount of money on the Negro schools. The convict labour contracts are a source of considerable revenue to the State; they make up . . . for most of the outlay for Negro education. . . . This convict labour is humanely treated; Mr. Fetters has the contract for several counties, and anybody who knows Mr. Fetters knows that there's no kinder-hearted man in the South. (75–76)

XIII   Peonage

Through Caxton's investigations Colonel French also "found that on hundreds of farms, ignorant Negroes, and sometimes poor whites, were held in bondage under claims of debt, or under contracts of exclusive employment for long terms of years—contracts extorted from ignorance by craft, aided by State laws which made it a misdemeanor to employ such persons elsewhere. Free men were worked side by side with convicts from the penitentiary, and women and children herded with the most depraved criminals, thus breeding a criminal class to prey upon the State"(229). The conditions of one Fetters labor camp, worse than any portrayal of slavery by Chesnutt, refute Appleton's words.[33] This kind of illegal operation, actually peonage, is also obviously a main source of Fetters's wealth. For about six dollars a month his agents buy the labor of a good plantation worker serving time; the cost of maintaining the prisoners, treated like cattle, is negligible. Bud Johnson's labor for eighteen months —with his life as a bonus—goes for little more than $100. Failure of the attempted reform is presaged in the inward speculation of Turner, manager of the local Fetters plantation, that Fetters " 'ain't goin' to let no coon-flavoured No'the'n interloper come down here an' mix up with his arrangements, even if he did hail from this town way back yonder' " (214).

Peonage, like disfranchisement, was a contemporary issue in which Chesnutt had more than fictional interest. He contributed an essay, "Peonage, or the New Slavery," to the September 1904 issue of a new Afro-American periodical, *Voice of the Negro*, in which he noted the flourishing of this "worse form of slavery" in Alabama and adjoining states. He identified "the development of the Negro," resulting "from greater learning and growing thrift and larger liberty," supported by "just laws impartially administered" as the only sure preventive of "slavery in some other form"; and for the meantime urged blacks to vote for candidates rather than for parties.[34] In the same essay Chesnutt explained that peonage was more acceptable in the South, where black slaves had previously labored for the exclusive benefit of white masters and pointed out that white children in southern cotton mills and foreign-born workers in northern sweatshops could be similarly oppressed under a corrupt political system.

XIV *Employment*

Chesnutt presents such conditions, which he clearly ascribed to personal prejudice as well as to criminal conspiracy, more graphically in his fiction. Old Peter in *The Colonel's Dream* tells Colonel French that he had worked for a railroad contractor and later had cut turpentine boxes in the pine woods until labor-related disabilities had made him expendable. Prevailing wages for Negroes in Clarendon, he also informs his former master, are " 'fifty cents a day, an' fin' yo'se'f, suh,' " that is, pay your expenses, work-related and otherwise. Even so, the liveryman in Carthage, the site of the Fetters cotton mill, feels that the Negroes are better off than the white women and children " 'from six years old up' " who receive from fifteen to fifty cents a day for twelve to sixteen hours of work under such deplorable conditions that half the youngsters " 'die of consumption before they're grown.' " French sees the situation for himself:

Through air thick with flying particles of cotton, pale, anaemic young women glanced at him curiously, with lack-luster eyes, or eyes in which the gleam was not that of health, or hope, or holiness. Wizened children, who had never known the joys of childhood, worked side by side at long rows of spools to which they must give unremitting attention. Most of the women were using snuff, the odour of which was mingled with the flying particles of cotton, while the floor was thickly covered with unsightly brown splotches. (114)

Hoping to benefit these workers, French begins building a model cotton mill—but for whites only. Whites object to his hiring blacks for its construction and are indignant at their getting equal pay for equal work. White bricklayers walk off the job when French makes the most efficient member of the crew, who happens to be black, their foreman. " 'We don't mind working *with* niggers, but we won't work *under* a nigger' " is their vocal reaction (191). The same attitude is expressed initially in "The Averted Strike," set in the Midwest. Likewise, in *The Marrow of Tradition* Dr. Miller is not properly respected by either the lay population or the white doctors. Jerry in the same novel knows that to continue as porter at the *Morning Chronicle* office he must forfeit his right to vote. In this work, too, Colonel Belmont favors driving some other Negro professionals out of town so that whites may get " 'the nigger business.' " According to Archie, the old Negro tailor in *The Colonel's Dream*, many black artisans have already lost their jobs due to the diversion of southern raw materials to the more highly industrialized North. In the Groveland (Cleveland) of "The Doll," Tom Taylor is aware that if he loses the lease on his barbershop in the Wyandot Hotel, no black person will be able to get it. Thus Chesnutt shows how a preponderance of economic forces arrayed against Afro-Americans makes their employment future bleak.

According to his writings, the job market did not change

substantially during his lifetime even in Cleveland, which was considered to have better than average race relations. The pattern set in his fiction through 1905 is apparent in his discussion of Negro employment in both "The Status of the Negro in the United States" in July 1912 and "The Negro in Cleveland" in the *Clevelander* for November 1930: a bulk of common laborers, a fast-diminishing number of skilled artisans, a few white-collar workers, a scattering of small businessmen being forced to retrench, and a minimal number of professionals serve an increasingly segregated minority. Blacks are shown to have made the largest employment gains in local and state government, a fact that Chesnutt attributed to their political power. The most blatant exclusion takes place in jobs controlled by labor unions.[35]

Chesnutt joined in the widespread protest against the decline in federal employment of blacks during the Wilson administration. He also appeared before a Senate committee in Washington on March 15, 1928, to argue against the reporting out of the Shipstead Anti-Injunction Bill. There he charged "baldly that the labor unions of the United States . . . are unfriendly to colored labor," citing twelve national unions which at the time made Negroes ineligible for membership. In further support of his charges, Chesnutt presented an affidavit from Clevelander Charles E. West, a licensed electrician, who had lost all his property, including his home, because of union policies. West was denied membership in the electricians' union, he could not get permission to hire union men, and his nonunion work was sabotaged.[36]

These are some manifestations of Chesnutt's strong conviction that "the Negro needs a better chance in the field of labor, the opportunity for more diversified employment, a chance to rise in the pursuits he follows . . . the common man's chance."[37] Sufficient means would, however, do more than improve the quality of life within the black community. According to Chesnutt, "When a Negro shall own or control a bank or a great business enterprise, I have not the slightest doubt that the board of directors will be willing to extend social courtesies to him. A prominent colored writer once said that one wholesale dry goods house or one great department store on Broadway would do more to combat race prejudice than all the race problem meetings that could be held in a year."[38]

XV *Education*

Chesnutt also believed that the extent to which an Afro-American could make the most of his chances for a fuller life through better employment depended largely upon his educational qualifications. Although education was a primary means of upward mobility to Chesnutt, as it was to most blacks of his time, he treated this issue less forcefully than white supremacy or voting, for example. This difference in emphasis may have been due to his belief that education alone would not solve the "Negro problem." He was aware that other Afro-Americans were promoting education for blacks more actively than those leaders were promoting minority sharing of other rights and privileges enjoyed by whites, and he recognized that Afro-Americans were receiving more education, despite its obvious inadequacy, than ever before in this country at a time when other vital rights previously exercised—voting, for example—were being increasingly denied to them.

Whatever the reason, Chesnutt's treatment of education is for the most part implicitly conveyed in his fiction. As has been shown in the preceding chapter, a significant number of his Afro-American characters demonstrate that they are educable and make profitable use of formal training on levels ranging from the industrial sphere, in the mode generally associated with Booker T. Washington, to the professional level, as urged by W. E. B. DuBois. In "Cicely's Dream," "The Bouquet," and *The House Behind the Cedars* many ex-slaves, freemen, and the offspring of both are "ignorant but eager" schoolgoers. Unfortunately, as shown in these selections as well as in "The March of Progress" and *The Colonel's Dream* particularly, these black seekers-after-education may attend only segregated public schools characterized by a shorter school term and different curricula, insufficient staff, and inadequate facilities. The one-teacher school operating for two months in a building serving other community needs is the rule. Poor whites in *The Colonel's Dream* are only slightly better off, for most of the public funds are deflected into use for private institutions. Without the political power to correct such inequities, public-spirited blacks in "The March of Progress" seek both to control and to help support their schools. Also, the great importance of education to Afro-Americans in the Clarendon of *The Colonel's Dream* is reflected in their enthusiastic reception of

Colonel French's verbal encouragement and offer of three dollars for every one dollar they " 'can gather, for an industrial school or some similar institution' " (161).

These fictional situations mirror the actual conditions of the times. Although Chesnutt was proud that, with the active support of enfranchised blacks during the Reconstruction period, North Carolina had maintained its leadership in public education in the South, he found segregated education distasteful in principle and disadvantageous—especially to Afro-Americans—in practice. He felt that either separate schools should be abolished or "the school fund should be fairly and equitably divided, and the same standard of efficiency maintained."[39] In his abbreviated reference to education in "Disfranchisement," Chesnutt scores the harmful psychological effects of separate school systems, which foster inferiority and superiority complexes in blacks and whites. In that essay as well as in a paper containing official statistics on salaries and per capita expenditures on education by race which he sent to Cable in 1889, Chesnutt confirmed the unfair allocation of public funds during the late 1880s. Under such a system blacks could get only inferior education, the skill and dedication of teachers notwithstanding.[40]

Though Chesnutt "maintained that race troubles would never cease until the Constitutional amendments were strictly observed . . . the color line entirely wiped out before the law, and equal justice and equal opportunity extended to every man in every relation of life," he suggested "education . . . as the most obvious and immediate palliative" for the race problem.[41] Elsewhere he stated that "the Negro's right to education is exactly the same as that of every other man. . . . The young should be educated as individuals and not as races or classes."[42]

In "The Status of the Negro in the United States" Chesnutt cited the educational system of Ohio as exemplary. "There are no separate schools, and in the schools colored children have equal rights and opportunities." Moreover, "Colored teachers" were employed in Cleveland, where "in the matter of scholarship [music and athletics] colored pupils often distinguish themselves." He contrasted "this democracy of the Cleveland schools," which many considered its "crowning glory," to "the Young Men's and Young Women's Christian Associations, also educational institutions, where . . . a person having more than a suspicion of color receives a very cold welcome, if any at all."[43]

Noting in "Liberty and the Franchise" that "the vast majority of colored people will remain for a long time hewers of wood and drawers of water . . . with profit and with honor to themselves," he observed further that the exceptional minority should be free to seek education to the full extent of their ability to learn.[44] Insofar as Chesnutt was concerned, race placed no limitation on that ability. Thus he was once again at odds with contemporary thought among influential, intelligent, and well-meaning white men who, as late as the early 1900s, pondered whether the Negro was truly educable and, if so, whether educating him would be in the best interest of the majority.[45] On the contrary, Chesnutt emphasized higher education as a criterion for the leaders of blacks. He also felt that those leaders should share the blood, the aspirations, and—to some extent—the fate of their followers. He believed too that "races should be judged by their best and not by their lowest, and a people who can produce a Frederick Douglass during slavery and a Booker Washington, a [Henry O.] Tanner and a [Paul Laurence] Dunbar within 30 years after emancipation, is worthy of the higher education."[46]

In summary, Chesnutt sought for Afro-Americans the same opportunities for education that he recommended for Africans in a letter of October 5, 1923, to Dr. Thomas Jesse Jones of the Phelps-Stokes Fund: "They need both [industrial and higher education], and not the one at the sacrifice of the other."[47] Thus, as on many other issues, Chesnutt took a position on education which reconciles certain aspects of the seemingly opposing philosophies of Washington and DuBois.[48]

XVI *Public Privilege*

But neither educational attainments nor social graces removed from Afro-Americans the stigma of color reflected in jim-crow practices which became increasingly legalized and widespread during the 1890s and well into the twentieth century. Chesnutt's emphatic treatment of such conditions perhaps reflects not only his distress at the worsening of race relations but also his resentment of the implied inferiority of blacks, both of which these developments denoted. Chesnutt could remember when there had been no legal separation of the races. After the Civil War many Negro Protestants had withdrawn voluntarily from white parent churches to form independent organizations (this was nothing new; the African Methodist Epsicopal Church had been organized in Philadelphia in 1778); public schools and army units were, on the whole, separate. However, there were no laws requiring either segregation or discrimination in all other areas of public privilege or civil rights. Moreover, according to the testimony of Thomas Wentworth Higginson, Sir George Campbell, native white South Carolinians, and Negro T. McCants Stewart, during the 1870s and 1880s blacks and whites received equal treatment and got along well in public places in the eastern seaboard states, in Louisiana, and even in Mississippi.[49] The Negro's weakened political and economic positions contributed to the changes which became noticeable in the 1890s in the North as well as in the South. A second factor was the gradual loss of both political and economic power to the "Straightout" or white-supremacy elements of the Southern Democrats by the aristocratic conservatives. And another was the attitude of the federal government toward some 8 million people of the colored races who came under U.S. jurisdiction as a result of the Spanish-American War:

The doctrines of Anglo-Saxon superiority by which Professor John W. Burgess of Columbia University, Captain Alfred T. Mahan of the United States Navy, and Senator Albert Beveridge of Indiana justified and rationalized American imperialism in the Philippines, Hawaii, and Cuba differed in no essentials from the race theories by which Senator Benjamin R. Tillman of South Carolina and Senator James K. Vardaman of Mississippi justified white supremacy in the South. . . . "No Republican leader," declared Senator Tillman, ". . . will now dare to wave the bloody shirt and preach a crusade against the South's treatment of the negro. The North has a bloody shirt of its own. Many thousands of them have been made into shrouds for murdered Filipinos, done to death because they were fighting for liberty."[50]

Until 1900 the only jim-crow law adopted by the majority of southern states applied to passengers aboard trains, which law South Carolina adopted in 1898, North Carolina in 1899, and Virginia in 1900. Nevertheless, many restrictions had been imposed on Negroes before that time, and the separate-but-equal Supreme Court decision in 1896 in the *Plessy* v. *Ferguson* case made matters decidedly worse for Afro-Americans. Chesnutt ascribed this trend to the disfranchisement of blacks, noting at the same time that the Negro was denied the protection freely accorded to any alien, who also had a government to whom he could appeal for redress when his rights were denied. At that time too Afro-Americans were generally held in such low esteem as social individuals that, as Chesnutt recalled in "Social Discrimination" in 1916, "a very distinguished writer and critic once wrote, in reviewing some of my own stories about people on the edge of the color line, 'We no more expect to meet them in our parlors than we would the lower animals.' "[51] He suggested the harmful effects of such an attitude in his Medina speech [1913]: "You all know from observation, what it means to be in a position where the finger of scorn can be pointed at one. It poisons all the fountains of life, especially if one is conscious of innocence and undeserved reproach. Put yourself in the position of an educated, intelligent, sensitive person of color, made to feel at every turn of life that he is an outcast, not entitled to courtesy and consideration, and you can imagine what a deterrent or deadening effect it must have upon the mind of such a man."[52]

Dr. Miller in *The Marrow of Tradition* is just such a personality. He is also the character Chesnutt uses to inveigh against segregated railroad accommodations, the kind of discrimination he wrote about most extensively. Returning to Wellington, Dr. Miller's chagrin at being ejected illegally from the first-class to the inferior jim-crow coach degenerates into mortification after he is unable to prevent McBane from using the coach as a smoking car, sees a Negro nurse with her mistress and "a Chinaman, of the ordinary laundry type," freely admitted to the better coach, and shares his accommodations briefly with a "noisy, loquacious, happy, dirty, and malodorous" group of black farm laborers, "fresh from their daily toil" (59, 60). The devastating effects of these encounters upon his psyche are suggested by Miller's wondering whether a dog brought into the coach by the Negro porter will be left there. The attitudes of both Dr. Miller and Dr. Burns, who had been sitting together initially, are expressed in the editorial comments of a Charleston, S.C., newspaper in 1885 that "it is a great deal pleasanter to travel with respectable and well-behaved colored people than with unmannerly and ruffianly white men"; and, in 1887, that "the common sense and proper arrangement . . . is to provide first-class cars for first-class passengers, white and colored."[53]

Chesnutt elaborated on the concurrent denial of the white man's rights and the threat of a proliferation of such regulations in "The Courts and the Negro," in his Medina speech (1913), and in "The Age of Problems." He also condemned discrimination in housing, in the armed forces, and in social intercourse in some of his writings, including "An Inside View of the Negro Question," "The Status of the Negro in the United States," and "The Right to Jury Service." The potential social, business, and political losses to black men because of their exclusion from normal channels of male white society led Chesnutt to comment, "The fate of nations has more often been settled in clubs and parlors than in courts and parliaments," and "many a valuable business or professional acquaintance is made around the social board or in the club room."[54] The inclusiveness of enforced separation of the races for social purposes is reflected in *The House Behind the Cedars* in Rena's letter declining to see Tryon clandestinely.

XVII   *The Church*

Likewise, Chesnutt stressed in his fiction the hypocritical practices of white Christian churches and indecencies to the dead in the name of racial segregation. As custom dictates, Mis' Molly Walden in *The House Behind the Cedars* sits in the balcony when she attends the Patesville Episcopal Church; Mammy Jane in *The Marrow of Tradition* and Peter in *The Colonel's Dream* grace the first floor of their "white folks' " church for the first time when the former witnesses little Dodie's christening and the latter is one of the principals in a double funeral. Sophy, a devoted pupil of the deceased Miss Myrover in "The Bouquet," is triply embarrassed by being excluded from her teacher's home, her church funeral, and her interment in the well-kept white cemetery. That place is a sharp contrast to the unkempt Negro graveyard in *The Colonel's Dream*. Clarendon mores decree that Peter be buried in this low and swampy place near the railroad track rather than in the French family lot. Violation of this custom brings final insult to the old man in his disinterment and unceremonious deposit on Colonel French's piazza during the night. This is an affront not only to the bereaved father but also to the memory of the little son for whom Peter had vainly sacrificed his life, for the child's last wish had been that the servant be buried near him. Chesnutt uses this incident to editorialize at length on "the color line . . . in all Southern towns [which] extend[s] on the surface from the cradle to the grave," explaining the psychology and difficulty of main-

taining a caste system among people who have never lived in the
relation of master and slave, and whose economic means and
social attainments become increasingly equal (262).

XVIII *Violence*

Friction resulting from efforts of whites to maintain the status
quo—to keep blacks in their place physically and psychologically—and opposing attempts by Afro-Americans to improve their lot in accordance with national tradition often
sparked violence. Chesnutt gives special attention to mob
violence and the lynching of blacks; the two often went hand in
hand. Though never directly involved in acts of violence, he was
deeply moved by their effects upon others, especially acquaintances and relatives. He was only nine years old when he had run
from his father's store in downtown Fayetteville to the Market
House, where Archie Beebe, a black man in custody and charged
with rape, had been fatally shot, as prearranged, by one of a
group of leading white citizens of the town.[55] In 1901 he included
Wilmington, North Carolina, in his tour of certain southern
states, to investigate the Wilmington Riot of 1898. Despite the
passage of time, he was still so incensed that many of the
witnesses he interviewed, including relatives, asked him not to
write about it. He did not heed their advice, but his tone is more
moderate than might have been expected from one who heard
from close kin firsthand accounts much more vividly remembered
then than when recounted sixty years later.

For three of Chesnutt's cousins, then young girls, the Wilmington Riot was a terrifying experience. Many of the Negroes
fled to the woods and swamps and others were hidden by whites
in their cellars, but their family (that of Dallas Chesnutt, a
brother of Andrew Jackson Chesnutt) remained in town when
tension mounted on November 9, 1898. The horror of the situation was lightened, however, by an audacious act: the girls'
brother Tommy, who was editor Manly's printer's devil, slipped
away from home that evening to the *Record* building and helped
to bury all the printing equipment after a mock funeral was conducted for it. Mrs. Fannie Headen, the eldest of the sisters, recalled
that she was at school the next day when, looking out a window, she saw white men carrying guns and marching "stretched
from sidewalk to sidewalk." She also heard one of them say,

"Let's throw a bomb in this nigger school [it was a private institution]!" The children, panic-stricken, ran to their white teacher's home nearby and got under the beds and between the mattresses. Mrs. Headen said too that their father, who was a railway mail clerk, was one of the few colored people able to get through the blockade that night; he saw much shooting along the railroad tracks.[56]

During the years between the Beebe lynching and the Wilmington Riot, such repression by violence had increased. The trend escalated to such an extent that in 1904 apologist Thomas Nelson Page wrote a mild article of protest.[57] According to the U.S. Bureau of the Census, over 2,000 Afro-Americans were victims of "the most abhorrent growth of the race problem" between 1885 and 1905.[58] Race riots also proliferated, in the South and in the North. Major outbreaks occurred in Statesboro, Georgia, and Springfield, Ohio, in 1904; in Atlanta, Georgia, and Brownsville, Texas, in 1906; in Springfield, Illinois, in 1908; and in Washington, D.C., Chicago, Illinois, and Longview, Texas, in 1919; and so many others within the year that James Weldon Johnson dubbed the hot months of 1919 "The Red Summer."[59]

That violence is a major element in much of Chesnutt's race-relations fiction from 1887 to 1925 is therefore hardly accidental. Throughout his lifetime the threat of violence was constant in the black community. It could erupt suddenly, without apparent cause, and with fatal results for innocent Afro-Americans. Thus Chesnutt's rationale for aggressive use of force by a stronger element—realistically white characters—ranging from profit-seeking slave masters like Mars Jeems in "Mars Jeems's Nightmare" through young pranksters in "Uncle Peter's House" to deliberate inciters of mob violence such as the "Big Three" in *The Marrow of Tradition*, is historically sound. However, Chesnutt's thematic treatment of these acts makes them morally indefensible and brands their perpetrators as culpable.

All the aspects of the lynchings and race riots presented in Chesnutt's writings are grounded in reality. The huge crowd in *The Marrow of Tradition* that had made all preparations to lynch Sandy Campbell, the mob in *The Marrow of Tradition* that destroys much Negro life and property in Wellington, and the smaller group in *The Colonel's Dream* that hustles Bud Johnson from his jail cell to painful oblivion are typical. The majority of them, "riffraff," are so engrossed in satisfying baser sensations and emotions that they overlook their roles as tools of more powerful, often respectable, members of the community who cannot afford to display their venality. In *The Marrow of Tradition*, for example, the sanctity of white womanhood is used by the "Big Three" as a front for white supremacy and Negro disfranchisement. Similarly, in *The Colonel's Dream*, Turner plays on the fears of insecure white blue-collar workers about economic and social equality for Negroes in order to insure their confederacy in killing Johnson after his first attempt has been thwarted. Thus declared ethical or altruistic motives often cloak maneuvers for economic or political advantage.

By showing the needlessness of such drastic action by these characters, Chesnutt diminishes them further. They are always superior in number, weaponry, and authority. At Fetters's labor camp French sees four Negroes ordered to overpower Bud Johnson, "throw him down with his face to the ground, and sit on his extremities while the overseer applied the broad leathern thong vigorously to his bare back," a procedure similar to the one used by overseer Nick Johnson to intimidate the slaves in "Mars Jeems's Nightmare" (218–19). In *The Marrow of Tradition* Watson, the Negro lawyer, informs Dr. Miller, returning to Wellington from a rural call, of the shocking turn of events: " 'The white people are up in arms. They have disarmed the colored people, killing half a dozen in the process, and wounding as many more. They have forced the mayor and aldermen to resign, have formed a provisional city government *à la française*, and have ordered me and half a dozen other fellows to leave town in forty-eight hours, under pain of sudden death' " (279).

Whites, however, already had complete control there as elsewhere in Chesnutt's fiction. Moreover, as already shown, the dispensers of justice are usually so color conscious that the relatively few blacks, including Bud Johnson in *The Colonel's Dream* and young Tom in "The Sheriff's Children," who commit offenses are assured of legally imposed punishment—if they can survive long enough to be tried; and the innocent, like Sandy in *The Marrow of Tradition*, are lucky if they are set free. The turn of events, in court and out, depends more on the character of the white authority figures than on any other single factor. Mob action can be curbed as well as catalyzed if the leadership so wills. In "The Sheriff's Children" the mob disperses after Sheriff Campbell shows that he will defend his Negro prisoner to the death.

Though not an officer of the law, Carteret in *The Marrow of Tradition* needs but a few hours not only to defuse the lynch mob but also to see that the "Wellington Grays, the crack independent military company of the city," are at the jail to protect Sandy (231).

Carteret could no doubt also have halted or at least considerably reduced the rampage of the mob which invaded the Negro neighborhood. Ironically, his shouted remonstrance, " 'Gentlemen! . . . this is murder, it is madness; it is a disgrace to our city, to our state, to our civilization!' " is construed as "encouragement and cooperation" (305, 306). Consequently, despite his belated good intentions, Carteret is, in effect, as much a party to violence as is the sheriff in *The Colonel's Dream* who makes no attempt to protect Bud Johnson from his executioners—"he never would have dreamed of shooting to defend a worthless Negro . . . who had declared a vendetta against the white race" (277). Though French tries to get the townspeople to prosecute the lynchers, who also whip all the Negroes they can find at the Dudley plantation for having harbored Bud, no one—not even the minister—will move in this case "upon the side of law and order." Peter's disinterment the next day forces French to decide: " 'The best people . . . are an abstraction. When any deviltry is on foot they are never there to prevent it. . . . When it is done, they excuse it; and they make no effort to punish it. So it is not too much to say that what they permit they justify, and they cannot shirk the responsibility' " (283).

XIX *Reaction*

In such a hostile environment Chesnutt seems to have favored various postures of nonaggression for the majority of Afro-Americans to give them better chances for psychological as well as physical survival. In order to cope with violence against which they have no adequate defense, his characters employ flight (Ben in "Lonesome Ben"), withdrawal (Viney in *The Colonel's Dream*), circuitousness (Solomon in "Mars Jeems's Nightmare" and Skundus in "A Deep Sleeper"), conciliation (Dr. Miller in *The Marrow of Tradition*), and resignation (Sandy Campbell in *The Marrow of Tradition*) with varying degrees of success.

Only a few exceptional characters follow extreme patterns of behavior—and they meet appropriate fates. Mammy Jane and her son Jerry in *The Marrow of Tradition* are capitulators. Although she is motivated altruistically by blind devotion to the daughter of her former owner and he selfishly by desire to keep his job and the approval of Carteret under any conditions, Chesnutt makes no distinction in his fictional judgment of them: swift dispatch by the bullets of whites, whom they had perceived as protectors. On the other hand, retaliatory violence by blacks is praiseworthy in principle, but—again realistically—never clearly successful. In *The Marrow of Tradition* Miller refuses to lead fellow blacks to certain defeat and death. A pragmatist, not a coward, he offers years of service rather than moments of fighting in a lengthy statement concluding: " 'My advice is not heroic, but I think it is wise. In this riot we are placed as we should be in a war: we have no territory, no base of supplies, no organization, no outside sympathy,—we stand in the position of a race . . . without money and without friends. Our time will come,—the time when we can command respect for our rights; but it is not yet in sight. Give it up, boys, and wait. Good may come of this, after all' " (283). Josh Green, already committed to sacrifice his life to avenge his father's brutal killing by masked Klansmen, welcomes the added incentive of defending the hospital. He will then be doubly justified in killing McBane. (That the riot provides a more acceptable means than premeditated assault is doubtless immaterial to Josh. However, regardless of provocation or intent, none of Chesnutt's Afro-American characters commits cold-blooded murder.) Like Green, other black male characters, including Isham in "The Marked Tree," Ben Davis in "A Web of Circumstance," Bud Johnson in *The Colonel's Dream*, and Tom Taylor's father in "The Doll," are so sorely tried that their manhood demands some expression of protest even at the risk of their lives. All are killed. Some, like Green, gain stature by dying.[60]

The philosophy dictating these actions appears in this excerpt from Chesnutt's "A Multitude of Counselors," in the *Independent*, April 2, 1891, when lynching was on the rise: "The colored people will instigate no race war. But when they are attacked, they should defend themselves. When the Southern Negro reaches that high conception of liberty that will make him rather die than submit to the lash, when he will meet force with force, there w ll be an end of Southern outrages."[61] Chesnutt also felt that such violent confrontations would be less likely to occur if mobs would not take the law into their own hands, if the law were enforced strictly and impartially, and if education and "the general spread of enlightenment" were fostered. In addition to writing about violence, Chesnutt supported the lengthy campaign of the NAACP to get a federal antilynching bill passed. On November 21, 1921, for example, he addressed identical letters to Ohio Congressmen Theodore E. Burton and Harry C. Gahn, asking them "to vote in favor of the Dyer Anti-Lynching Bill," which NAACP Secretary James Weldon Johnson had persuaded Representative L. C. Dyer of Missouri to introduce in the House that year.[62]

XX *Public Opinion*

Chesnutt's high regard for the prestige and power of the law has been documented repeatedly. For him, however, public opinion was potentially a greater force in implementing or nullifying the effectiveness of specific laws. Moreover, inasmuch as many laws inimical to Afro-American interests were being enacted in the South during Chesnutt's most active writing period (1885–1905), he believed that their "chief hope for the speedy and peaceful recognition of [their] public rights at the South [lay] in the united and aggressive public opinion of the North."[63] Obviously, marshaling of a good opinion depended greatly on the appeal of the black public image. Consequently, Chesnutt was especially sensitive to the coverage of blacks by the media, which then consisted primarily of newspapers, periodicals, and bestselling books; and he monitored them on behalf of all Afro-Americans.

XXI *The Press*

Chesnutt pointed out how most of the white people who controlled publications capitalized on news unfavorable to blacks. Often the items were deliberately slanted, facts supporting the Afro-American position were suppressed, and the language intentionally pejorative. If the alleged wrongdoer was black, his racial identity was always played up nationwide (Chesnutt found the emphasis on race particularly repugnant); if he was vindicated, the item—if reported at all—was relegated to a few lines on an inside page. Editorial approval of regulations and social attitudes inimical to blacks was common. Achievements or protests by blacks were largely ignored. "One student of the subject [observed] that in order for the Negro to break into print, he had to 'break into a house, break his neck or break some law.' "[64]

Chesnutt provides classic examples of such misuse of the press in the figure of Major Carteret in *The Marrow of Tradition*. In his drive to achieve white supremacy politically and to financially benefit himself and his partners, Carteret, through inflammatory articles in the *Chronicle*, encourages whites to lynch Sandy Campbell before he can be tried for the alleged rape-murder of old Mrs. Ochiltree. When Sandy is suddenly cleared, Carteret is mainly concerned about the credibility of his paper. Later he uses a previously discarded editorial in the black newspaper to provoke such a hostile reaction in the white community that the blacks will be afraid to vote in the upcoming election.

Chesnutt had been told about the use of a similar tactic by the editor of the Fayetteville *Observer* in 1888[65] and was no doubt also aware that Josephus Daniels had done likewise with the [Raleigh, N.C.] *News and Observer* during the disfranchisement campaign. Daniels is quoted as having admitted in 1944 that his paper's " 'partisanship was open, fierce, and sometimes vindictive, and was carried in news stories as well as in editorials. . . . Whenever there was any gross crime on the part of Negroes, the *News and Observer* printed it in a lurid way, sometimes too lurid, in keeping with the spirit of the times. . . . We were never very careful about winnowing out the stories or running them down . . . they were played up in big type.' "[66] Varying degrees of political as well as of the racial bias which Chesnutt deplored are evident not only in the coverage of the election and the Riot by the *News and Observer* (pro-Democrat and antiblack) but also in the *Wilmington Evening Dispatch* (pro-Democrat and antiblack), the *Clinton Caucasian* (pro-Populist), the *New York World* (neutral), and the *Indianapolis Freeman* (problack).

Chesnutt often felt impelled to express his disapproval of the editorial policies of Northern publications, as in his letter of July 28, 1903, to the *Outlook* for its approval of suffrage restriction in the South and one of April 20, 1923, to Charles T. Henderson, editor of *Cleveland Topics*, about an article critical of black and white male students sharing dormitory facilities at Harvard.[67] On the other hand, in "The Courts and the Negro" he praised "the staunchness of the New York *Evening Post* and the *Independent*, which . . . amid all the ruck of concession and compromise have kept alive the torch of liberty against the day when . . . the Negro shall 'take the rank of a mere citizen . . . and when his rights as a citizen or a man are to be protected in the ordinary modes by which other men's rights are protected.' "[68] Of much greater significance to the public concept of Afro-Americans was Chesnutt's supplying the documentation which forced the Macmillan Company to withdraw William H. Thomas's *The American Negro* from the market in 1904.[69]

To the extent that normal contacts between blacks and whites became more proscribed by segregation, the press gained in its influence to determine public opinion about Afro-Americans. Perhaps Chesnutt had this in mind in July 1903 when he wrote DuBois:

What the Negro needs more than anything else is a medium through which he can present his case to thinking white people, who after all are the arbiters of our destiny. How helpless the Negro is in the South your own writings give ample proof; while in the North he is so vastly in the minority in numbers, to say nothing of his average humble condition, that his influence alone would be inconsiderable. I fear few white people except the occasional exchange editors read the present newspapers published by colored people.[70]

In 1914 Chesnutt became a member of the Press Committee of the NAACP. Thus he tried by presenting in many ways a more realistic, positive black image to the public through various media, to mold the public opinion which he often felt was the black man's best hope for improving his lot.

XXII *Group and Personal Esteem*

Chesnutt was also concerned about improving, in a more subjective manner than was appropriate in his fiction, the Afro-American's opinions of himself both as a member of a particular ethnic group and as an individual human being. He wished to counteract directly the psychologically destructive effects of negrophobia which shadowed every black in the United States—to try to allay as much as possible the trauma of the "twoness" which DuBois experienced and the threeness which had plagued Chesnutt during his youth.[71] "Meekness and humility," he explained to the Wilberforce University literary societies in "Race Ideals and Examples" (1913), "is a fine trait of character, if not carried to the point of servility, or beyond the point of self-respect. There is a danger of going too far in that direction, or, in seeking a proper attitude toward the world, of going too far the other way. The happy medium, the attitude of respect for the rights and feelings of others, and of demanding with firmness and courtesy the respect of others for your own rights and feelings, is the most desirable one." Chesnutt carefully differentiated between "race pride" and "race self-respect:

. . . you and your forbears have suffered so severely from race pride as to make it doubtful whether that particular quality is a virtue. No man derives any merit from his birth; it is only what he does that counts; and while it is pleasant and valuable as a spur to effort to contemplate a long record of achievement in one's ancestors, it is no ground for demanding respect or consideration from others."[72]

In his biography of Frederick Douglass and many shorter pieces, Chesnutt cited numerous blacks worthy of emulation. Among them were Alexander Dumas *père et fils*, Crispus Attucks, Peter Salem, Robert Small, John M. Langston, J. W. Hood, Guillon Lethiérè, Blanche K. Bruce, Alexander K. Pushkin, Hiram Revels, Robert Browne Elliott, Joseph C. Price, all those nameless ones who fought to make America victorious in battle from the time of the Revolution, and countless others who had struggled just as hard for success on all levels in a segregated society. The majority of these men were self-made, a category which Chesnutt admired greatly and which, in one of his earliest speeches, "Self-Made Men" (1882), he praised highly for having achieved despite a dearth of opportunity and advantage. In that speech he challenged his audience to emulate such examples in a land where "the highest positions [are] within the reach of the lowest."[73] His, too, was the American Dream—modified.

In a 1915 speech he declared, more temperately, that rights and opportunities for blacks could be secured only by their "making the best use of every industrial and professional opportunity and by the cultivation of a sound morality. There is no royal road to freedom and to opportunity; they must be fought for with every available weapon. With freedom and opportunity once secured, I venture that equality, in the broadest sense of the word, equality of capacity and of achievement will become less of a theory and more of an established fact."[74] When, in 1928, it was obvious that Afro-Americans were still second-class citizens, Chesnutt reaffirmed his belief in the capability of blacks. He found that in spite of being "Jim-Crow-ed from the cradle to the grave . . . the colored people are doing very well . . . and, given the start they have, the only thing which can keep them down is the prejudice of white men."[75]

He continued to hold that "humanity is above race—it is a much bigger thing to be a man than to be any particular kind of man, and the time will come when it will be a bigger thing to be an American than to be any particular kind of American. . . ." He clung to the belief that "most [whites] are good people and anxious to do the right thing as they see it. All we can do is to try to make them see it as we do, to maintain the principle of equal rights and equal opportunities to all men, with equal rewards according to their deserts, and to so conduct ourselves and so develope [*sic*] and use the power, intellectual, political, industrial and spiritual, that is latent in ten millions of people that it will be impossible to longer deny them these equal rights and opportunities."[76]

Chesnutt strove forthrightly to ground his basic themes, the humanity of the Afro-American and man's inhumanity to man, in the events and issues of his time. He believed, as he wrote Booker T. Washington on November 3, 1906, "that this race problem involves all the issues of life and must be attacked from many sides for a long time before it will approach anything like a peaceful solution," which, though influenced by blacks, would have to be determined ultimately by whites.[77] Finally, he prophesied in *The Marrow of Tradition* that the Negro Question "will trouble the American government and the American conscience until a sustained attempt is made to settle it upon principles of justice and equality" (92).

CHAPTER 7

Style

Fine thoughts must be clothed in worthy words before they become available for the use of the rest of mankind. The "mute, inglorious Miltons" do not move the world. Only when our best thoughts have passed laboriously, and painfully for the most part, through the loom of language, and have been submitted to the gauge of rhyme or reason, or both, and have been put into such shape that they will convey to the wayfaring man something of the same impression that they made upon the mind that first conceived them—then and only then do they rise to the dignity of literature.[1]

CHESNUTT's position on many controversial issues of his day was more in keeping with post-1950 than pre-1920 public opinion, but his style—including certain techniques—keeps him astride the turn-of-the-century line. Much of his literary philosophy, however, is timeless. His fiction, his essays, and his speeches from 1881 through 1930 show the impact upon Chesnutt of the exhortations of the great masters of Western oratory from Demosthenes to Abraham Lincoln and Frederick Douglass (all great favorites of Chesnutt); of the musings of essayists as different as Montaigne and Addison and Steele; of his own study of rhetoric and logic; and of his listening to black preachers and storytellers.[2]

I *Rhetoric*

Chesnutt's style is decorous. In exposition his propositions are clear, his arguments logical and ordered. His narratives vary in structure, but all are free of extraneous material. Whether simple and direct or Ciceronian, his sentences flow. Also properly varied in length and structure, they reflect an effective use of antithesis, alliteration, assonance, balance in thought and construction, climax, repetition of words or phrases for effect, and similar endings. Chesnutt clarified his ideas with allusions, examples, quotations, and aphorisms—the latter sometimes in the language of origin followed immediately by an English translation. (For one who had so little formal education or informal guidance, the range of his reading is astounding.)

The following quotation from a 1913 speech, "The Relation of Literature to Life," contains several of the stylistic devices just mentioned—especially antithesis:

Now, as over against *this* life we have had set for us the life to come, and history, I am afraid, teaches that our good friends the preachers, who have done so much for us, have, in magnifying the life to come, at least in past ages, neglected this world unduly; and while they were building up an elaborate system of hells and heavens and purgatories beyond, have permitted castes and creeds to work untold horrors among men on earth; while they paved the streets of heaven with gold, they left men to wade through earthly mud; while angels soared through the skies, tired men and women trudged on foot, or rode on the backs of weary beasts. But men finally waked up to the importance of life here, and now we have steam and electricity and improved sanitation, and professions of human equality—I presume we shall work around to the fact of it in due course of time. Our good ministers, however, do not let us forget the other life, which it is well we should not be unmindful of. But after we have heard all the sermons and read all the books, when sickness comes to us, and death threatens, all the delights of heaven fade into insignificance before the touch of solid earth and the sight of four plastered walls. Your yearning is not for the streets of gold, but for the asphalt pavement. You prefer the street-cars to the wings of the morning. The sound of a familiar voice is sweeter than the music of the celestial choir; you would rather feel the touch of a loved hand than the sustaining arms of the angels as they waft your soul to glory. One ray of sunlight is worth more to you than the splendid radiance of the heavenly city. Such is the law of life. Whether a boon or a burden, a blessing or a curse, we cling to it, and thus we seek, and should seek, to make of it, for ourselves and others, the best that it is capable of becoming.[3]

One device he used often in his nonfiction to emphasize a point or to introduce a note of levity was a sudden shift from standard or literary usage to the vernacular, which, as is usually true of black folk speech, often has figurative elements. Discussing the number and status of Afro-Americans in "Age of Problems" (1906), Chesnutt declared: "Taking our nation in the raw, and finding in its present population the ingredients of our future

race, ours is a mixed race already—combined of every variety of
mankind under the sun. Some are taken with a wry face—the
Negro is a hard pill to swallow. The Chinese we have sought to
keep out—the Negro is too big to throw up." In his letter of
November 3, 1906, to Booker T. Washington, Chesnutt continues
the thought in the same metaphorical framework: "The American people will have to swallow the Negro, in punishment for
their sins. Doubtless the dose is a bitter one, but there is no other
way out. It only remains for all of us to make the process as little
painful as possible to all concerned."[4]

II   *Influences and Similarities*

Chesnutt seems to have patterned aspects of his works after
writers he admired, while at the same time individualizing his
fiction. Like Sir Walter Scott, he exhibits a penchant for the past,
for a central romantic involvement, and for meticulous attention
to detail. Like Cooper, Stowe, and Harte, he finds nobility in
seemingly ignoble characters. Like William T. Thompson, T. B.
Thorpe, and Mark Twain, he leavens the faults and foibles of all
classes of men and of American society as a whole with humor,
satire, and irony. Like Howells, he is extremely circumspect in ex-
ploring physical relationships between the sexes, but unrelenting
in exposing social ills while seeking ethical cures. Like Turgenev,
Chesnutt champions the cause of the slave with a pronounced use
of the dramatic method, associated with the Russian writer; and
like Dickens, Stowe, Tourgée, and Cable, crusades for oppressed
elements of society, whether bound or free. Like Joel Chandler
Harris, Thomas Nelson Page, and Cable, he explores hierarchal
relations between whites and blacks in the South before and after
the Civil War. Like Sarah Orne Jewett, Hamlin Garland, Mary
N. Murfree, Kate Chopin, and all the other local colorists or
regionalists, he brings a particular geographic area to life on his
pages and preserves its contemporary culture for posterity. Like
Dickens and Lamb he ventures successfully into fantasy; and like
Henry James, finds the mental and emotional states of his
characters sometimes more suspenseful than their observable actions. James, incidentally, is the only imaginative writer whose
techniques—as opposed to subject matter and thematic
treatment—Chesnutt expressed in writing a desire to imitate. His
Journal V contains two short sketches written "a la Henry

James," with emphasis on point of view and psychological probing of character.[5] Such marked psychological treatment of character in many later stories, notably of Dave in "Dave's Neckliss," Tom Taylor in "The Doll," Ben Dudley in *The Colonel's Dream*, and Rena Walden/Rowena Warwick and George Tryon in *The House Behind the Cedars*, is a creditable reflection of James's influence.

Unlike James, Howells, and Zola, Chesnutt tried neither to create new literary forms nor to develop a body of critical theory to undergird his fiction. He should nevertheless be considered more a creative innovator than a slavish imitator. By giving free rein to his imagination within these bounds in pursuit of his twin aims of personal artistic expression and promotion of the Afro-American cause, he distinguished his work in many ways. Among other things, Chesnutt adapted some of the popular fictional forms of his day—the frame story and the folktale, for example—to effect social change. He measured his success ultimately in terms of his writings' appeal to the reading public as much as to their meeting critical standards. Chesnutt sought to write literature of quality, which at first he believed that readers would appreciate despite its controversial themes. The latter he never considered changing, for throughout his literary career Chesnutt followed his "old rule—to write for art's sake . . . the truth as I saw it, with no special catering to anybody's prejudices."[6]

III   *Temper*

Consequently, Chesnutt cannot be neatly labeled as a Classicist, Romanticist, Realist, or Naturalist. Some of his early short sketches, such as "A Busy Day in a Lawyer's Office" and "A Soulless Corporation," are in the tradition of Theophrastus and La Bruyére. "The Kiss" and "Her Virginia Mammy" afford the love interest and happy endings typical of romantic fiction of the age, the latter of which Chesnutt more often than not refused to supply. "The Origin of the Hatchet Story," "A Midnight Adventure," and all of the Uncle Julius stories with marvelous elements also fall within the Romantic category. However, the Uncle Julius tales which show the slaves unable to cope with their environment as well as those short stories and novels with black and/or white characters doomed to fail because of forces such as race and class prejudice have Naturalistic aspects. Paradoxically, these aspects become increasingly apparent in the novels, with their post-Emancipation settings.

Even in *The House Behind the Cedars*, which reflects the Romantic temper in its emphasis upon individuals and their emotions, John Walden/Warwick, George Tryon, and Rena Walden/Rowena Warwick are adversely affected by sociological forces. Rena's death, culminating the novel, may be viewed as the final reaction of a woman of her background, temperament, and experience to the harsh socioeconomic realities of the age. This tragic end is as inevitable though perhaps not as consciously self-willed as the decision of Isabel Archer Osmond in Henry James's *Portrait of a Lady* to continue her blighted life and of Maggie in Stephen Crane's *Maggie: A Girl of the Streets* to end hers. Rena, a sensitive creature who had been reared in the genteel Southern tradition of dependence, seems to have lost the will to live after having been subjected to the psychological pressures of race and sex, clearly delineated in the novel, all her life. Her death suggests their enormity.

By and large, however, most of Chesnutt's fiction is so grounded in reality and so balanced in its portrayal of both admirable and offensive human qualities that he may perhaps best be categorized as a Realist with a penchant for psychological treatment of character. That Chesnutt is basically a Realist is supported by a certain consistency in treatment of setting, character, and plot typical of the Realistic temper. As has already been indicated, the times and places of his fiction are true to life and so exactly detailed that they are easily identifiable. The characters, predominantly middle- and lower-class, engage in routine activities or cope with mundane problems in the manner of ordinary rather than exceptional individuals. As in life, they are neither all good nor all bad, though a few like Becky in "Sis' Becky's Pickaninny," Henrietta Noble in "The March of Progress," Mr. Ryder in "The Wife of His Youth," Wiley in "Dave's Neckliss," Laura Wharton in "A Grass Widow," Colonel French in *The Colonel's Dream*, McBane and the Delameres in *The Marrow of Tradition*, and Rena Walden, Frank Fowler, and Jeff Wain in *The House Behind the Cedars* come near to exemplifying one or the other of these extremes. Further, most of Chesnutt's characters both succeed and fail in the course of the action of the novels.

In depicting the seamier side of life, Chesnutt reflects a

preference for decorum, expressed in a letter of June 29, 1904, to W. H. Page: "As a matter of personal taste I shrink from the sordid and brutal, often unconsciously brutal side of Southern life—as I should from the shady side of any other life."[7] Like Howells, he presented many such episodes "in a broad and suggestive way, without disgusting detail," but nevertheless with enough direction and intensity to make his point.[8]

Thus, both because of personal inclination and a desire to avoid accusations of bias through sensationalism, Chesnutt seldom details physical assaults of any kind. Instead of describing floggings of slaves, Uncle Julius usually states tersely that they got "fo'ty," meaning forty lashes on their bare backs. The depiction of the thrashings of the "noo nigger" (the master has been temporarily transformed into a slave) in "Mars Jeems's Nightmare" and of itinerant laborer Bud Johnson in *The Colonel's Dream* is exceptional. Perhaps Chesnutt hoped that the immediacy of the erstwhile slave's suffering would evoke more empathy from white readers. It certainly illustrates grimly the Old Testament law of retribution—even if only for a few days.

On the other hand, no specific is furnished when, in "The Dumb Witness" (obviously the original or a prior version of the Viney–Malcolm Dudley episode in *The Colonel's Dream*), Malcolm Murchison beats his slave housekeeper-concubine, Viney. Having found out that Viney's revelation of their relationship to a prospective bride has caused his jilting, he threatens:

"I will teach you . . . to tell tales about your master. I will put it out of your power to dip your tongue in where you are not concerned."

There was no one to say him nay. The law made her his. It was a lonely house, and no angel of mercy stayed his hand.[9]

IV *The Intrusive Author*

Whether the use of implication as a technique is more effective than explication depends upon the reader, now as then. Authorial comment, of which the last portion of the quoted passage is an example, was a device widely used during the early nineteenth century and is now often associated with Thackeray, whom Chesnutt admired greatly as a writer. In such statements the writer is forthright and subjective, though not usually as impassioned as

Chesnutt in his plea on behalf of Rena and John in *The House Behind the Cedars*:

> If there be a dainty reader of this tale who scorns a lie, and who writes the story of his life upon his sleeve for all to read, let him uncurl his scornful lip and come down from the pedestal of superior morality to which assured position and wide opportunity have lifted him, and put himself in the place of Rena and her brother, upon whom God had lavished his best gifts, and from whom society would have withheld all that made these gifts valuable. To undertake what they tried to do required great courage. Had they possessed the sneaking, cringing, treacherous character traditionally ascribed to people of mixed blood—the character which the blessed institutions of a free slave-holding republic had been well adapted to foster among them; had they been selfish enough to sacrifice to their ambition the mother who gave them birth, society would have been placated or humbugged, and the voyage of their life might have been one of unbroken smoothness. (116–17)

V   *Point of View*

Whether or not by design, Chesnutt balanced much of his understandable partisanship for his black characters by an effective use of point of view which at the same time heightened suspense in the development of plot. Thus, despite his fervor, he was able to maintain enough objectivity in his fiction to have credibility among openminded white readers. Chesnutt used omniscience sparingly, preferring in the novels particularly to shift the point of view from one character to another. In most cases he penetrated their consciousness only superficially. However, his occasional revelation of thought processes in a manner anticipating the stream-of-consciousness technique utilized by many later writers is impressive. He also favored an active or observant narrator in the majority of his short pieces, sometimes resorting even to the use of diary entries.

Another, more complex use of point of view is apparent in the frame stories. In them Chesnutt presents different points of view with such skill that the careful reader gains a totality of insight based on a weighing of the testimony of all the main characters involved but denied to each of them. This subtle revelation of tensions lends an artistry to the Uncle Julius tales unmatched by the seemingly similar recollections of Uncle Remus as told by Joel

Chandler Harris. Moreover, in these tales as well as in many other pieces of fiction Chesnutt achieved an exceptional objectivity: neither Uncle Julius, John, nor Annie can be said to express Chesnutt's views altogether. As a result, some readers of *The Conjure Woman*—among whom were a number of individuals who believed blacks incapable of such creativity—insisted that he could not be an Afro-American.

VI   *Techniques of Characterization*

Chesnutt's careful attention to and facility in handling of character may stem from his belief that "nowhere is the kinship of humanity to divinity more apparent than in its power to create out of thin air, creatures who live and breathe and love and hate and do and die,—and yet live on forever."[10]

A. Names

He took special care, like Dickens, to suggest the personality or status of many of his characters by their names. The implications in tag names such as Attorney Sharp and all the other individuals in "A Busy Day in a Lawyer's Office," Wiley in "Dave's Neckliss," Peter Gump in "The Prophet Peter," Henrietta Noble in "The March of Progress," Archibald Straight in *The House Behind the Cedars*, Letlow and McBane in *The Marrow of Tradition*, and William Fetters in *The Colonel's Dream* are obvious. The aristocratic connotations of Rowena and Warwick, names assumed by Rena and John Walden in *The House Behind the Cedars* when they are passing for white, will be more apparent to students of nineteenth-century English literature and history.

Moreover, readers who recognize George Tryon's surname as that of the Royal Governor of North Carolina (1765–1771) who built the lavish official residence called Tryon's Palace and was finally forced out because of his tyrannical rule, have their concept of George as an aristocrat reinforced. That the fictional Tryon is also fallible may be more than coincidental, given Chesnutt's meticulous care in naming his characters. Major Carteret's name has similar significance: Sir George Carteret was one of the first Lord's Proprietors of Carolina (the territory now comprising both North and South Carolina) under charters granted by Charles II of England in 1663 and 1665. Again, characters with last names of Campbell, McNeal, McNeill, McDonald, McMillan, McRae, McDougald, and McLean celebrate families from the Scottish highlands who settled in the Cape Fear area by 1767. People of such ancestry comprised the majority of the Nordic population thereabouts during Chesnutt's time. Furthermore, families with the same names as Chesnutt's characters were living in Fayetteville and nearby when Chesnutt's works were first published, and many were pleased to see them in print. Uncle Julius McAdoo and Sandy Campbell, ex-slaves, are examples of freedmen who, having no knowledge of their ancestral names, followed the widespread practice, after Emancipation, of using the last names of their former owners.

B. Description

Descriptions of many Chesnutt characters are pithy, often poetic. Jeff Wain in *The House Behind the Cedars* is " 'a shifty scoundrel . . . jes' a big bladder wid a handful er shot rattlin' roun' in it.' " Rowena is called a "sweet flower of womankind" by her fiancé; Frank sees her as "a dove with a wounded wing" after her engagement is broken. At that point in the novel Chesnutt calls her "a very Niobe of grief." (The last example illustrates Chesnutt's copious use of allusion in his writings; he made most frequent use of Greek and Roman classics, and the Bible.) Though these depictions are exact, others are occasionally misleading, depending upon the perception and/or intent of the informant. If supplied by other characters they are sometimes revelatory of the latter. To his onetime rival, Tom in "Tom's Warm Welcome" " 'was a pore shote.' " Peter Gump in "The Prophet Peter" " 'ain't got sense enough to come in out of the rain.' " A gossip in *The Colonel's Dream* sees Ben Dudley as " 'only a poor stick, the last of a good stock run to seed.' " Both Tryon's vulnerability and his biased outlook are evidenced by his spate of anger at John and Rena, "who had surprised his virgin heart and deflowered it by such low trickery."[11]

In *The Marrow of Tradition* Chesnutt underscores the subordinate and defenseless position of most Negroes in Wellington during the riot when, at the sight of Dr. Miller's buggy, "half a dozen men and women . . . with fear written in their faces

. . . made a dash for cover, disappearing, like a covey of frightened partridges, in the underbrush along the road" (275). Such apprehension could hardly have been felt by old Mrs. Polly Ochiltree in the same novel, who in early life "had been accustomed to impale fools on epigrams, like flies on pins, to see them wriggle." In her dotage she inflicts pain on fools and friends alike (21).

C. Development

Realistically, most of Chesnutt's characters remain basically the same; only a few develop noticeably. In the latter category Rena Walden/Rowena Warwick in *The House Behind the Cedars*, Clara Pemberton in *The Marrow of Tradition*, and Graciella Treadwell in *The Colonel's Dream* become more understanding and appreciative of others after having had emotional problems themselves. Mars Jeems (for James) in "Mars Jeems's Nightmare," an exception, changes radically. His turnabout is clearly attributable to his ordeal of living for a time as a slave through an extraordinary metamorphosis which tinges the tale with romanticism. This short piece, slightly reminiscent of Kafka's "Metamorphosis" but happier in its resolution, strikingly illustrates Chesnutt's adaptation of literary techniques for his particular ends—in this case to induce even white readers to empathize completely with the black slave.

D. Attitudes

Chesnutt used the epigram effectively to speak for himself, to make authorial comment, and to express the views of a character. Commenting on his "new novel" (*The Marrow of Tradition*), race relations, and violence in the United States in a letter of October 8, 1901 (shortly after the assassination of President McKinley), to Booker T. Washington, Chesnutt wrote metaphorically: "The country is suffering from blood-poisoning, and the South is the source of the infection."[12] In a more literary, philosophic manner he observed in *The Marrow of Tradition*:

Selfishness is the most constant of human motives. Patriotism, humanity, or the love of God may lead to sporadic outbursts which sweep away the heaped-up wrongs of centuries; but they languish at times, while the love of self works on ceaselessly, unwearyingly, burrowing always at the very roots of life, and heaping up fresh wrongs for other centuries to sweep away. (239)

Conversing with Rena in *The House Behind the Cedars*, John Warwick reacts more emotionally to the same subject: " 'God is too often a convenient stalking-horse for human selfishness. If there is anything to be done, so unjust, so despicable, so wicked that human reason revolts at it, there is always some smug hypocrite to exclaim, "It is the will of God" ' " (163).

E. *Internal Turmoil*

Chesnutt had a penchant for using the thoughts and emotions of his characters as major elements in their portrayal. Such usage is noteworthy, especially in view of the tendency of most other contemporary writers to depict blacks more or less simplistically. Chesnutt was also somewhat *avant garde* in following James's stress on psychological aspects of character. Only the reader is privy to the fierce battle between revenge and responsibility in Tom Taylor's mind; even Judge Beeman, observant as he is, has no conception of the nature or extent of the suppressed emotion which Taylor evinces only slightly. Likewise, no other characters in *The House Behind the Cedars* know how much George Tryon suffers after repudiating Rowena. He seems never thereafter completely free of the anguish he experiences during the long night hours following their fatal confrontation. The full extent of the psychological damage to Dave in "Dave's Neckliss" and Viney in *The Colonel's Dream* becomes apparent only after his insanity and suicide and her last conversation with Malcolm Dudley.

On the other hand, in *The Colonel's Dream* Chesnutt artfully externalizes the explosive build-up of pride, poverty, lovesickness, and jealousy within Ben Dudley through his having to wear to the Assembly ball a black cutaway "not of the proper cut, too short in the sleeves, and too tight under the arms" (203). Attempting to drown his frustrations in drink but winding up full of self-pity and harmless belligerence makes Ben a more believable, appealing character.

All in all, Chesnutt's careful attention to and facility in handling of character no doubt stems from his perception of character as "perhaps the most important element in a work of creative imagination."[13]

VII *Plot*

Chesnutt seemed not to find plot as significant as character in the creative process though he conceded in "The Writing of a Novel" that the plotless novel is in reality no more than a character sketch:

Unless written with exceptional charm of expression or upon some theme of immediate and compelling importance a novel must have such a dramatic movement, such an unfolding of events, such a play of characters, and such uncertainty of outcome as to hold the reader's attention through four hundred solid pages of reading matter.[14]

He was less able to meet these criteria in his novels, although he repeatedly demonstrated his mastery of the shorter forms of fiction before receiving from both Cable on *The House Behind the Cedars* and Walter Hines Page on *The Colonel's Dream* advice and encouragement on developing the various elements of the novel. Chesnutt apparently had no trouble developing *The Marrow of Tradition*, which is the most highly plotted of his three novels. However, he noted in a letter of June 8, 1928, to Harry C. Block of A. Knopf Publishers that he "pruned, padded and polished, etc." all of his works.[15] Some of this diligence is reflected not only in Chesnutt's fairness to the reader in supplying all the leads in the course of the development of a story to justify the sometimes surprise ending popularly attributed to O. Henry (who began publishing too late to influence Chesnutt) but also in the occasional intriguing irresolution of an ending. This is obvious in "A Deep Sleeper," but less apparent in *The House Behind the Cedars* and *The Marrow of Tradition*.

VIII *Mood*

The outcome of most of the tales, many of the short stories, and some incidents in the novels is suggested by the settings, which in turn help to establish the mood. Frequently the elements play important roles in this process. Thus by noon of the day that Uncle Julius tells the "harrowing" ghost story in "The Gray Wolf's

Ha'nt," "the rain had settled into a dull, steady downpour. The clouds hung low, and seemed to grow denser instead of lighter as they discharged their watery burden, and there was now and then a muttering of distant thunder" (*The Conjure Woman*, 162). Again, appropriately, Uncle Julius unfolds the love tragedy in "Hot-Foot Hannibal" on a road in a "dark and solemn swamp [crossed by an] amber-colored stream flowing silently and sluggishly . . . like the waters of Lethe [permeated by] the heavy, aromatic scent of the bays, faintly suggestive of funeral wreaths . . ." (*The Conjure Woman*, 203).

When, in *The House Behind the Cedars*, Rena gets lost in the pine forest while fleeing from Tryon and Wain, she is terrified not only by the growing darkness, the swampy terrain, the prickly underbrush, and the black snake but also by "the soughing of the wind through the swaying treetops" as part of the sudden storm punctuated also by lightning, thunder, and "the crash of falling timber" (244, 245). In sharp contrast, when on the following morning Frank comes along the road which Rena had almost reached before collapsing the night before, the scene is idyllic. A careful review reveals that Chesnutt used the same outdoor setting in both "Hot-Foot Hannibal" and *The House Behind the Cedars*, but varied his emphasis and the atmospheric conditions to create predetermined variations for different effects.[16]

IX *Figurative Language*

Another distinctive feature of Chesnutt's style is his use of figurative language, which sometimes is downright folksy and at other times poetic in its beauty, intensity, and compactness. And always it is functional: to vivify setting, to heighten mood, to round out character, to help describe or propel the action, to explain attitudes, to clarify ideas.

Chesnutt's towns and cities have qualities to which they live up—or down, as is often the case. According to John, the narrator of the tales in *The Conjure Woman*,

there brooded over it [Patesville] a calm that seemed almost sabbatic in its restfulness, though . . . underneath its somnolent exterior the deeper currents of life—love and hatred, joy and despair, ambition and avarice, faith and friendship—flowed not less steadily than in livelier latitudes.[17]

In *The Colonel's Dream* the once-elegant gate entrance, the green lizard on a defaced post, the rattlesnake in the carriage track bordered by rank grass and weeds, the boarded-up and glassless windows of the weatherbeaten two-story Georgian "mansion," and the haphazard hillocks and hollows in the bare yard adjacent to it concretize the marked decline of the Dudleys. The seeming seat of authority is the "massive oaken armchair" occupied by old Malcolm at one end of the long piazza, in contrast to the "straight-backed chair" in which Viney sits at the other end.

On another note, perhaps the sheer horror of Bud Johnson's lynching in *The Colonel's Dream* (and the corresponding rise in such violence in real life) inspired Chesnutt, as author, to a transcendent metaphorical lyricism in his abbreviated treatment of that climactic moment:

A rope, a tree—a puff of smoke, a flash of flame—or a barbaric orgy of fire and blood—what matter which? At the end there was a lump of clay, and a hundred murderers where there had been one before. (277)

X   *Symbolism*

Although the characters in most of Chesnutt's fiction are believable, a few of them seem also to serve as symbols in short allegorical sequences. Among them are Ben in "Lonesome Ben," Malcolm Dudley and Viney in *The Colonel's Dream*, Mr. Ryder and 'Liza Jane in "The Wife of His Youth," and Colonel French and Laura Treadwell in *The Colonel's Dream*. Through Ben, Chesnutt shows in sequence the aesthetic appeal of black skin tones and the opposite effect of a "yaller" complexion—contemporary color standards notwithstanding. Ben may also be seen as a symbol of the vilified free mulatto, who had no firm place in the Southern slave economy. Driven to run away by his master's dire threats and consequently cut off from friend and foe alike, Ben eventually suffers a complete loss of identity and dies. This chain of events suggests the psychological damage to any individual denied a positive role in the society of which he is a part.

Dudley and Viney may be seen to represent white-black relations before and after Emancipation. The drama they act out illustrates how the slave Viney is initially antagonized by the self-centered behavior of her all-powerful owner. After Emancipation the same struggle continues to the detriment of both: he, still seeing her only as a means to an end (now money) and she deliberately thwarting him out of revenge. This episode may easily be interpreted as an implicit plea for better understanding—including acceptance of both responsibility for and forgiveness of past wrongs—and cooperation between the races in the South for their common good.

The center of the short story "The Wife of His Youth" is intrarace relations, happily a resolution of problems between the free person, symbolized by Mr. Ryder, who has had advantages and made the most of them in order to rise in the North, and the freed person, represented by illiterate and uncultivated 'Liza Jane, in whose heart concern for her long-lost husband still reigns supreme. Mr. Ryder's voluntary identification of himself as the Sam Taylor the older woman has been seeking and reinstating her as his wife in front of his cultured Blue-Vein friends provide a pattern of behavior which no doubt Chesnutt hoped more advantaged blacks would follow. Their recognizing the cardinal virtues of less fortunate blacks would facilitate better cooperation of the two groups for solving common problems.

In *The Colonel's Dream* an equally desirable reunion of the North and South, represented by Colonel French and Miss Treadwell respectively, to their mutual advantage, is thwarted by reactionary elements of entrenched power (William Fetters particularly) and racism. Colonel French seems ideally suited for his role: Southern-born, he appreciates the traditions of the region and wishes only to effect changes which he thinks are desirable for both ethical and economic reasons. (Symbolically, he has already put away the sword he carried into battle for the South.) However, some of the poorer whites, like Jim Greene, insidiously influenced by the existing power structure and crippled by a creed of racial superiority, deny themselves benefits which would accrue to blacks less extensively. Laura, recognizing her own limitations and fearing that neither she nor French can make the adjustments required for them to live together happily above or below the Mason-Dixon line, releases him from their engagement. Their going their separate ways seems to reflect Chesnutt's mounting conviction that the race problem in the South would remain unsolved for the foreseeable future.

XI *Wit and Humor*

One of the most pervasive aspects of Chesnutt's writing is his humor, which ranges widely from the simply amusing through the ludicrous and satirical to the ironic. In a letter of June 5, 1890, to Cable, he explained: "Almost everything I have written has been humorous, and I had thought that I had a rather keen sense of humor" despite conditions of life which inclined him to be otherwise.[18] The foibles as well as the flaws of mankind are the butt of Chesnutt's humor, but understanding his meaning often requires careful reading. Sometimes his incisive wit masquerades as banter; sometimes, too, the satire is subtle and the irony lies in the inflection of a word or phrase.

XII *Banter*

Chesnutt resolved early not to "record stale Negro minstrel jokes, or worn-out newspaper squibs on the 'man and brother.' "[19] Contrary to popular practices, he was gentlest with the ordinary black folk, as in "A Limb of Satan." In this light piece he makes acceptable Uncle Ebenezer's turnabout from annoyance at and condemnation of the "limb of Satan" to affection for and indulgence of the mischievous little Sammy when he finds out that the child is his grandson.

"The Fall of Adam," largely a sermon by an uneducated but resourceful freedman preacher, is an example of the tall tale in the Old Southwest tradition. Adam's fruitless flight from God around the world and through space affords the peculiar pleasures which Americans seem to take at seeing others experience minor discomfort, physical and otherwise. This selection may also be read as a folk sermon, a nature myth, a satire on miscegenation, and a "why" story. The latter, an amusing account for the beginnings of almost everything, was a prime favorite among Negro folk during the nineteenth century.

More down to earth, but having the same perverse appeal, are the episode in *The Marrow of Tradition* in which Sandy thinks he sees his "ha'nt" and the hilarious climax of "Stryker's Waterloo," in which Napoleon Stryker loses his chance to receive unprecedented cash damages for injuries he allegedly suffered in a railroad accident three years before. Stryker had not been as badly hurt as he claimed, and during the series of court battles has had trouble continuing to look and act like an invalid. Now hobbling along on crutches down a narrow street en route to the courthouse to hear the jury's verdict, known to be in his favor, he simultaneously hears the cry " 'Mad dog! Run for your lives!' " and sees coming at him a big black dog with bloodshot eyes, barking and foaming at the mouth. People on the street begin to stampede, but Stryker, dropping his crutches, outstrips all of them, including the doctors, lawyers, witnesses, the trial judge, and the railroad claim agent, in sprinting past the courthouse and up a tree. The case is thereafter speedily settled out of court, with the plaintiff receiving only a pittance of what the jury would have otherwise awarded him.

Among other short stories similarly amusing are "How Dasdy Came Through" and "Tom's Warm Welcome." Both have satirical overtones about religion, courtship, and class distinctions. However, the ludicrous description of Lee Dickson, a hotelkeeper in *The Colonel's Dream*, is downright ridicule of "the custom in the south, to consider labor dishonorable." Among other eccentricities, Dickson keeps a horse and buggy standing in front of the hotel all day so that he may ride to get a shave at the barber shop next door and go other places nearby.[20]

XIII   *Satire and Irony*

Satire, of which some trace can be found in most of Chesnutt's work, becomes more biting in "A Matter of Principle" and a model of subtlety in "Baxter's Procrustes." In the first he scores color prejudice among blacks; in the second, extreme dilettantism among affluent whites. "A Matter of Principle" concerns the prosperous Groveland Blue-Vein family of Cicero "Brotherhood" Clayton, who does not practice what he preaches about the brotherhood of man, especially in his relationships with dark-skinned Afro-Americans. Because of this bias his daughter, Alice, loses the catch of the season, a U.S. Congressman. "Baxter's Procrustes," through a hoax played upon the aesthete members of the Bodleian Club, suggests the fallaciousness of making value judgments on the basis of superficialities or outside appearances and shows the speciousness of arguments made to justify such judgments. This general criticism is applicable not only to the

Claytons but also to Mis' Molly Walden's Patesville circle in *The House Behind the Cedars*, who find Frank Fowler socially unacceptable because he has neither a fair skin nor straight hair. Except for Rena, these Blue Veins do not learn the lesson which events in the narratives clearly teach. Their lack of sensitivity is especially ironic because all of them have been more or less victimized by American race prejudice, based mainly upon color.

The irony comes through from another angle in "Her Virginia Mammy." Clara Hohlfelder, adopted when a small child by German immigrants, would consider herself unworthy of Dr. John Winthrop, who can trace his ancestry to the *Mayflower*, if she knew that her mother had been a slave. This makes no difference to Winthrop, who encourages her to believe all her forebears were white aristocrats so that the two may marry, although he knows that the mulatto who Clara thinks is her "Virginia mammy" is actually the young woman's mother.

George Tryon's attitude toward Rena is just the opposite: he breaks their engagement as soon as he finds out that her beauty is "tinted." Since the reader is aware of Rena's racial antecedents from the outset, many of George's thoughts and statements about her prior to this disclosure are ironic. During their short engagement, George does not get the import of Rena's wondering aloud whether he would marry her if she were her young nephew's mulatto nurse. The irony is compounded when Rena interprets Tryon's unqualified affirmation to mean color instead of class, as he intended. To him,

she represented in her adorable person and her pure heart the finest flower of the finest race that God had ever made—the supreme effort of creative power, than which there could be no finer. . . . To mention a Negro woman in the same room where he was thinking of Rena seemed little short of profanation. (*The House Behind the Cedars*, 90, 103)

With slavery as depicted in Chesnutt's fiction and as criticized in his other writings, the reference in *The House Behind the Cedars* to slavery times as "the good old days" in the mention of Liberty Point as a place where slave auctions were sometimes held is also ironic. The great difference in the way slaveowners and slaves perceived their mutual relationship is the basis of much of the irony in Chesnutt's fiction about the pre–Civil War period. In "Tobe's Tribulations," when one of the McSwayne slaves, after having successfully run away and gotten established in the North, writes back and encloses a bill for his twenty-odd years of labor—

"Mars Marrabo cusst en swo' des tarrable, en ole missis 'mos' wep' fer ter think how ongrateful dat nigger wuz, not on'y ter run 'way, but to write back sich wick'niss ter w'ite folks w'at had alluz treated 'im good, fed 'im, en clothed 'im, en nussed 'im w'en he wuz sick, en nebber let 'im suffer fer nuffin' all his life." (*Short Fiction*, 99)

However, in "The Passing of Grandison," another satire about such tunnel vision, Colonel Owens is shocked into awareness that his estimate of the intelligence, ingenuity, and loyalty of his slave Grandison has been all too low when the slave refuses many opportunities to become free while in the North only to return to the Kentucky plantation and engineer the escape of his family and fiancée. Moreover, the resultant irony of situation, which does not become apparent to the reader until the dramatic denouement, greatly enriches this short story.

In "Sis' Becky's Pickaninny," after Uncle Julius has revealed that "Kunnel Pen'leton" has already bargained to trade Sis' Becky for a race horse and knows that the horse trader will not take her baby too, Uncle Julius explains:

"Kunnel Pen'leton did n' wanter hu't Becky's feelin's—fer Kunnel Pen'leton wuz a kin'-hea'ted man, en nebber lack' ter make no trouble fer nobody,—en so he tol' Becky he wuz gwine ṣen' her down ter Robeson County fer a day er so, ter he'p out his son-in-law in his wuk. . . ." (*The Conjure Woman*, 142)

Whether Uncle Julius is being naive or ironic here cannot be determined, but the statement is implicitly ironic. A rare exception in which "the southern situation is worse [now] than in the days of slavery," according to ironist Chesnutt, is voting: "then three-fifths of the slaves, counted as property, were at least represented in the congress; now, when [all Negroes are] counted, they are not represented at all."[21]

The difference between the perceived—usually the expected—and the actual mode of behavior of major characters in *The House Behind the Cedars* and *The Marrow of Tradition* particularly supplies additional irony. In *The House Behind the Cedars* George Tryon, as the victorious knight in the annual tournament of the Clarence Social Club, chooses Rowena Warwick as the Queen of Love and Beauty. Moreover, he is a model of southern gallantry throughout their courtship and engagement—until he finds out about Rena's mixed blood. Subsequently he pursues her most unchivalrously until she dies. On the other hand, ex-slave Frank Fowler is consistently the chivalric knight from the time that he saves the child Rena from drowning until the adult Rena breathes her last.

Ironically, too, Frank's trappings are so humble and he performs the ritualistic duties of a knight in such a self-effacing manner that this role may be overlooked. He is content to worship from afar. His trips to South Carolina may be seen as quests on behalf of his lady. At the tourney, though he does not enter the lists, he is wounded because of the intentness of his search for Rena. His mule and "kyart" instead of a spirited horse and a bandanna instead of a lady's dainty handkerchief denote his humble state; the sharp contrast accentuates the nobility of his character.

In *The Marrow of Tradition* Dr. Miller maintains his professional standards and tries to serve his community; Major Carteret uses both his profession and his community to promote his personal interests. Having thus betrayed his ideals more than he intended, it is ironic that Carteret's plea—" 'Gentlemen! . . . this is murder, it is madness; it is a disgrace to our city, to our state, to our civilization!' "—to end the violence at the Negro hospital is misinterpreted as encouragement by the mob to kill the blacks and burn their community. It is ironic, too, that both Mammy Jane and her son, Jerry Letlow, faithful servitors of whites, who have promised to protect them, are killed by whites—Jerry while waving a white handkerchief as a flag of truce.

The assertion that old Mrs. Ochiltree's then unknown assailant is "a brute in the lowest human form" becomes ironic with the discovery that her assailant was aristocratic Tom Delamere. The disclosures that both Mrs. Ochiltree and her niece, Mrs. Carteret, southern ladies, are guilty of fraud, and that, on the other hand, Mrs. Miller is legally Mrs. Carteret's half-sister, have all the impact of the unexpected opposite. In *The Colonel's Dream* the finding of the coroner's jury that Bud Johnson, the victim of a lynch mob, committed suicide, has a macabre twist.

In his writings Chesnutt demonstrates that he is so versatile a stylist that he cannot be neatly categorized. Rather, as an artist he ably used a variety of writing and artistic techniques—ranging from down-to-earth folk to lofty literary—to provide a body of writings remarkable for their breadth and felicity of expression.

CHAPTER 8

Triumph and Defeat

To have one's achievements recognized by one's own people [is] a very great pleasure.[1]

CHESNUTT's fiction, though often controversial, commanded public attention internationally and won widespread critical approval for its artistry. His nonfiction has received little critical attention. His readers, in Great Britain, Switzerland, and Australia as well as from "Maine to California," were relatively few in number considering the quality of his work. This lack of popularity was due primarily to his choice and treatment of subject matter, which increasingly and more overtly concerned controversial—sometimes explosive—contemporary issues. One reviewer of *The Marrow of Tradition* astutely observed that "the writer who tries to treat these difficult themes in any other than a sensational way may not hope to number his readers by the hundreds of thousands, but he can find a large reward in the appreciation of discerning souls."[2] In the same vein, an advertisement of *The Wife of His Youth* in the *Cleveland Leader* for December 13, 1899, had forewarned prospective buyers that the book deserved "something more than careless reading." These statements apply as well to most of Chesnutt's writings.

I Reception of The Conjure Woman and The Wife of His Youth and Other Stories of the Color Line

The Conjure Woman, comprised of seven Uncle Julius stories, was both the most popular and the most highly praised of Chesnutt's six major works despite—or in some cases because of—the failure of many readers, including some critics, to perceive the subtleties of Uncle Julius's character. Uncle Julius was too completely equated with Harris's Uncle Remus, as is

clearly indicated in several of the quotations from newspapers
and periodicals in the brochure "Charles W. Chesnutt in Plat-
form Readings."[3] Walter H. Page, then editor of the *Atlantic*,
and John S. Durham, an Afro-American attorney and sugar plantation manager, were among the more discerning in praise of the
volume, with Durham emphasizing Chesnutt's making his blacks
"real live natural human Negroes and not the creations of the
books."[4] Both the black Reverend George W. Henderson and
white Mary Tracey Earle admired Uncle Julius. In addition to
her glowing review, Earle wrote Chesnutt that "the turning of all
the stories to the advantage of Uncle Julius . . . gives the last
delicate half tone to your picture."[5] In "Novel Notes," *Bookman*,
June 1899, Florence A. H. Morgan reacted similarly, declaring
also that "we [whites] have viewed the plantation Negro from
every side but his own, which is here shown in a manner which
furnishes evidence of its truthfulness."[6] Conversely, the uniden-
tified reviewer of *The Conjure Woman* in the *Critic* for July 1899
reluctantly acknowledged the selfishness of Uncle Julius's
motives, declaring that the revelation "leaves a bad taste in the
mouth." That essayist preferred the more stereotyped "old-time
Negro character rounded out and made complete by . . . little
touches of sympathy and appreciation . . . and humor."[7] Moreover, the anonymous contributor to "More Fiction" in the *Nation*, June 1, 1899, held that the tales "lose in effectiveness"
because of "the deep policy imputed to their relator."[8] Obviously,
critical judgment here is impaired by preconceptions which the
essayists were either unable or unwilling to relinquish.

William Dean Howells was more objective and more scholarly
in his evaluation of both *The Conjure Woman* and *The Wife of
His Youth.* After pointing out minor deficiencies in certain stories
in *The Conjure Woman*, Howells determined that "Mr. Chesnutt
seems to know quite as well what he wants to do in a given case as
Maupassant or Tourguénief, or Mr. James, or Miss Jewett, or
Miss Wilkins, in other given cases, and has done it with an art of
kindred quiet and force. . . . Character, the most precious thing
in fiction, is as faithfully portrayed against the poetic background
as in the setting of the Stories of the Color Line." Continuing,
Howells admitted ignorance of the ways of black citizens: "We
had known the nethermost world of the grotesque and comical
negro and the terrible and tragic negro *through the white
observer on the outside* [emphasis mine] . . . but it had remained

for Mr. Chesnutt to acquaint us with those regions where the paler shades dwell as hopelessly, with relation to ourselves, as the blackest negro."[9]

More empathetic, Carolyn Shipman concluded "The Author of 'The Conjure Woman,' Charles W. Chesnutt"—in which she also alludes to some of his other stories—comprehensively and prophetically:

He treats a difficult subject delicately and with the skill of an artist. In all his work he faces the problems of the race to which he in part belongs, and treats them with the critical ability of the lawyer, yet with that degree of partisanship which tempers justice with mercy. Underneath the humor and light touch of some of his stories is a tragic vein, sometimes lightened to pathos, and a philosophy which make his sincerest admirers feel that Mr. Chesnutt's best work is still before him. A writer whose philosophy of life is constructive, and not destructive, can safely count on the future.[10]

Horace Traubel also praised Chesnutt highly. Chesnutt's artistic use of indirection, his adherence to historical fact, his display of psychological insight, and his moral forbearance make his stories "better than sermons," according to Traubel. "Writing like Chesnutt's is mediatorial. Chesnutt stands on the borderline reassuring the doubters [*sic*] both sides. . . . You do not need to go to the negro with dates and sums in arithmetic. You need to go to the negro with soul. Soul will take you to the negro and give him to you. . . . And Chesnutt is soul."[11] Chesnutt evidently approved of these and other reviews of his works in "The Conservator," for the dedication he enclosed in a letter of October 20, 1907, to Traubel to go in the latter's copy of *The Colonel's Dream* reads: "I love to have you read my books, because you read them with my eyes—and with my heart."[12]

II *Mixed Reaction to* The House Behind the Cedars *and* The Marrow of Tradition

Traubel's views had been anticipated in part when Chesnutt was designated "Laureate of the Color Line" in the December 9, 1899, issue of the *New York Mail and Express*. In works published thereafter, Chesnutt strove more directly to quicken his readers' "moral curiosity." Paradoxically, the aggressiveness which has since enhanced his literary stature destroyed then his chances of pursuing a literary career as he had hoped. At the time

(1900–1905) most of his black and some of his more liberal white readers praised his three novels highly, but white reaction as a whole became more hostile. Various reviewers noted that *The House Behind the Cedars* displayed Chesnutt's "philosophical reasoning," "his sincerity, simplicity, and restrained expression of deep feeling," and his "keen sense of dramatic effect."[13] This novel, cited as rich in incident and in suggestion, was also found enthralling and realistic.

According to "Charles W. Chesnutt's First Novel," a review in the *Cleveland Plain Dealer*, November 4, 1900, "the case is presented with the impartiality of a judicial statement and is left to the judgment of the great jury of readers. . . . As the presentation of a profound and perplexing problem of American life, it is of masterly ability." Adopting a different stance sociologically, the *Nashville American* commented succinctly that "while the book teems with fine writing and a masterly handling of incident, yet it is a wanton attack upon something that the South holds sacred."[14] Also in this vein, the *Brooklyn Eagle* of December 1, 1900, questioned Chesnutt's judgment in choosing such a theme. "The 'color line' is too deeply ingrained in the hearts of the people of this generation for a story of wrong and suffering of the sort described by Mr. Chesnutt to bring forth any response to its appeal. The conditions portrayed may be imagined, but it is a fair query whether they really could exist."[15]

As the mixed reaction to *The House Behind the Cedars* had portended, sales did not reach expected levels. However, the editorial staff of Houghton Mifflin were so impressed by the literary quality of *The Marrow of Tradition* that they anticipated offsetting any financial loss which might accrue from the slow sale of the three volumes already published by the firm.[16] Regrettably, the response of most of the white readers was so reactionary that neither the zeal of Chesnutt supporters nor the publisher's vigorous sales promotion could make up the difference. Anticipating this, Frank T. Barnett, a friend employed in the Illionis State Attorney's Office in Chicago, wrote Chesnutt on November 5, 1901:

Unfortunately for you, from a financial viewpoint, no less than that of a literateur, the subject of your excellent work is not one that will commend it to the general public. The truths you portray so faithfully are unwelcome . . . the indifference in the white people, resulting from the influence of the unwelcome facts, is not compensated for by that large measure of appreciation, which these works merit among colored people.[17]

Most blacks who bought or read the novel *The Marrow of Tradition* were enthusiastic. Charles E. Lane wrote Chesnutt on January 5, 1902, that he had read all Chesnutt's other volumes of fiction, which he "considered equal in every way to . . . Charles Dickens's best books [but] you have written my book at last—'The Marrow of Tradition.' It is an ideal work of what some people call fiction, but I have not read so much truth out of any book save the Bible. Your last book is a masterpiece and you have more completely portrayed therein the real conditions in the South and set forth more precisely the actual relationship existing between the races than any writer who has undertaken the job since Mr. Lincoln issued the Emancipation Proclamation."[18]

Afro-American Charles W. Anderson, a New York politician who in 1905 became Collector of Internal Revenue for the Wall Street District of New York City, had expressed similar sentiments in correspondence to Chesnutt on December 11, 1901, citing the climactic confrontation of Major Carteret and Dr. Miller at the latter's home as an " 'eye-moistener'. . . . The race owes you a debt of gratitude for the great service you are rendering it, and every intelligent member should see to it that this book is brought to the attention of the makers of public sentiment in this country."[19] He himself was already doing so. Chesnutt sent copies to President Roosevelt and Congressmen Edgar Crumpacker, C. E. Littlefield, Marlin E. Olmstead, and John B. Corliss as well as to former Representative W. H. Moody, who had recently been appointed Secretary of the Navy. Francis J. Garrison, on the Boston staff of Houghton Mifflin, was likewise trying "to induce others to read it." Finding that Chesnutt's "fairness . . . great restraint . . . rare skill and discrimination . . . very dramatic and effective climax" warranted favorable comparison with Mrs. Stowe's technique in *Uncle Tom's Cabin*, Garrison declared the book "by far the best and strongest thing that [Chesnutt has] done yet."[20]

Reviews in the *Nation* of March 20, 1902, and the *Richmond Times* (n.d.) were also typical of favorable critical reaction. The latter stated:

The power of such a book as Chesnutt's *The Marrow of Tradition* lies in its searching truthfulness. Dealing as this book does with matters over which there is deepest feeling, its value must depend upon the fidelity with which it portrays the conditions. To the accuracy of the picture Mr. Chesnutt has presented, there is a surprising unanimity of opinion. The riot he describes might have been photographed in a dozen Southern towns; the murder has, unfortunately, been reduplicated a score of times, and even the minor details and atmospheric effects of the book carry with them the conviction of actuality.[21]

In sharp contrast, the *Independent* for March 6, 1902, carried "a notice" which Chesnutt found "not only unjust . . . to the book, and to my motives, but . . . personal to the point of offensiveness."[22] The *Wilmington Messenger* for January 19, 1902, was more libelous:

Chesnutt is a Negro who loves to hate the whites in the South and to malign them. . . . [*The Marrow of Tradition*] does not stop at exaggerations. . . . It is a book of falsehood, slander, and malice. "The Bookman" is too candid to laud and magnify the work of such a liar and defamer.[23]

The race issue appears even to have affected the objectivity of veteran William Dean Howells, who judged the book "less excellent in manner" because it was "less simple." He also held that the novel "would be better if it was not so bitter," but at the same time justified Chesnutt's stance both historically and psychologically. Moreover, Howells found Chesnutt's aesthetics and ethics sound. Howells was most obviously contradictory, however, in declaring on the one hand that in the "republic of letters . . . all men are free and equal," but on the other hand that Chesnutt, having always performed at his worst at "the higher average of the ordinary novelist . . . ought always to be very much better, for he began better, and he is of that race which has, first of all, to get rid of the cakewalk, if it will not suffer from a smile far more blighting than any frown."[24]

III *Chesnutt's Dilemma*

Chesnutt, deeply shaken by such adverse criticism, presented the dilemma to his publishers:

I would like your opinion . . . as to my being able to write a book dealing with the color line from my point of view which would be likely to make a popular success . . . enough to produce a modest return for the amount expended in writing it. It is true that I have not been writing primarily for money, but with an ethical purpose entirely apart from that; yet I have always hoped that I might perchance strike a popular vein, for, unless my books are read I shall not be able to accomplish even the ethical purposes which I have in view.

I am beginning to suspect that the public as a rule does not care for books in which the principal characters are colored people, or with a striking sympathy for that race as contrasted with the white race. . . . If a novel which is generally acknowledged to be interesting, dramatic, well constructed, well written—all of which qualities have been pretty generally ascribed to "The Marrow of Tradition". . . cannot sell 5,000 copies within two months after its publication, there is something radically wrong somewhere, and I do not know where it is unless it be in the subject.[25]

Houghton Mifflin evidently agreed. The editors praised his writing ability, which the *National Cyclopaedia of American Biography* in 1904 affirmed in noting that critics had ranked Chesnutt "among the foremost storytellers of the time."[26] Nevertheless, the company declined to publish *The Colonel's Dream* because it had lost money on both *The House Behind the Cedars* and *The Marrow of Tradition*. As a consequence, Chesnutt's last published novel carried the imprint of Doubleday Page, and that largely because his friend Walter H. Page was now a partner. In a letter congratulating Chesnutt on an early version of it, Page informed him that "a distinguished Southern writer [with] a full quota of Southern prejudices" found *The Colonel's Dream* "a most touching story."[27] Moreover, Dr. William Hayes Ward, editor of the *Independent*, found the novel sufficiently interesting to break his non–novel reading habit and to hold his attention until he finished it.[28] Alice E. Hanscom, editor of the *Reading Circle*, complimented Chesnutt for "keeping alive the light by which men may discern the conditions they have inherited and the responsibility resting upon themselves to better those conditions. I don't quite see how you can so successfully keep the impartial, unimpassioned tone."[29]

IV *Public Rejection of* The Colonel's Dream

Shortly after publication of the novel, Chesnutt notified I. F. Marcosson, on the staff of the publishers, that the most appreciative reviews have come from the South. They disagree with my conclusions, they deprecate the publication of the book, but they treat it with respect and do not deny its correctness as a picture of widespread conditions. That the conditions are widespread is indicated by the fact that the story has been variously located in the Carolinas, Georgia, and in Alabama.[30]

Despite Chesnutt's having avoided the more inflammatory issues of intermarriage and miscegenation, and having permitted only the most approved personal relations between the races in *The Colonel's Dream*, the book did not sell and public reaction still varied greatly. The *Nashville American* for October 9, 1905, found *The Colonel's Dream* to be a "bitter, passionate arraignment of the white people of the south in their treatment of the Negro [which] does not contribute in any way to a solution of 'the problem.' " On the other hand, according to the *Charleston* (South Carolina) *News* for October 29, 1905, "this book deals with the old theme of race in the south, but it is handled by a writer with more tolerance than usual. There is little bitterness here. It is an honest attempt to understand the southern point of view." More laudatory, the London *Southern Guardian* for November 8, 1905, concluded that "no novel of modern times has better directed our attention to the racial problem of the southern United States than has this one. Yet the purpose of the book is artfully concealed in a story that has many interesting features." On December 2, 1905, the London *English Review* reported that "either as a political pamphlet or a novel [*The Colonel's Dream*] makes exciting reading. Although Chesnutt has a definite purpose in telling the story, he has not forgotten the novel, which belongs to the better school of American writing." E. J. Lilly, a white former resident of Fayetteville, later found the book so pleasing and "superior to anything that Thomas W. Dixon ever wrote" that he initiated correspondence with Chesnutt in 1916, despite the fact that the two had been out of touch for more than thirty years.[31]

V *Out of the Mainstream*

Although all but forgotten by white readers and literary critics during the intervening years, Chesnutt remained preeminent as an Afro-American author in black literary circles. He also became better known among blacks as a whole because of his uncompromising advocacy of equal rights for Afro-Americans. His zeal for a then seemingly hopeless cause is implicit in his "eulogistic" but nevertheless reliable biography of Frederick Douglass. The critical reviews of this work were—and continued to be— generally favorable.[32] Published responses to Chesnutt's essays, already shown to be largely concerned with contemporary race-related issues, were more nearly reactions than reviews. The stance of the respondents was usually based more on previously held positions than on considered judgment of the information presented. Though many opinion-makers rejected Chesnutt's conclusions, some cited him for his clarity, coherence, restraint, and—sometimes—provocativeness.[33]

Editors of Afro-American periodicals continued to solicit Chesnutt for stories and essays; he published several in the *Crisis*, the organ of the National Association for the Advancement of Colored People. Chesnutt was held in such high esteem that, in 1927 and later, when DuBois was editor of the *Crisis*, cash awards called Charles Waddell Chesnutt honorariums went annually to the three young black creative writers found most promising by a panel of judges. The impetus provided by this kind of popularity and the resurgence of literary creativity among blacks during the 1920s, sometimes called the Harlem Renaissance, helped facilitate a new edition of *The Conjure Woman* in 1927.

VI *Ethnic Evaluation*

A review of subsequent criticism requires an ethnic qualification: as a rule, when white American literary critics after Howells and through the 1940s deigned to recognize Afro-American authors, they usually lumped them together regardless of basic differences in their literary fortes (Chesnutt in fiction and Dunbar in poetry, for example), rather than compare them with white authors in the usual literary categories, such as genre, locale, historical or literary period, temper, style, and the like. According to John Hope Franklin (*From Slavery to Freedom*), of all the Negroes writing during the late nineteenth century Chesnutt "made the greatest impression."[34] Other twentieth-century observations about his skill support this assessment. "The first Negro to write the short story and the novel, aware of the techniques of these literary forms as genuine art," Chesnutt put imaginative prose writing by blacks on a sound aesthetic basis and elevated the plane of Negro authorship.[35] Alain Locke, a premier Afro-American critic of the 1920s, gave Chesnutt and Dunbar credit jointly for the "historic breakthrough of the Negro author into the mainstream of American letters."[36] Vernon Loggins (*The Negro Author in America*), commenting on Dunbar's *Folks from Dixie*, published nearly a year before *The Conjure Woman* became available, stated that Dunbar "never attained Mr. Chesnutt's mastery of treating a folk tale from a subtle and intellectual point of view" or in writing "bold and uncompromising fiction on the Negro problem." [37] Loggins also held that the advent of *The Conjure Woman* "was positive evidence that Negro literature was coming of age."[38]

Chesnutt's rank as the best Afro-American writer of tales and short stories went unchallenged through the 1930s. Many critics found *The Conjure Woman* to be his "best book," rivaling or overshadowing Joel Chandler Harris's Uncle Remus tales. DuBois chose "The Wife of His Youth" as "one of the best short stories there is," while Loggins, Blyden Jackson, and George E. Kent are among the scholars who gave "Baxter's Procrustes" first place within and without a racial context. Through the 1930s Chesnutt was generally considered "the best" and "the best known" Negro novelist in the United States, being superseded thereafter by Richard Wright with his *Native Son*. William Stanley Braithwaite, an Afro-American critic, in 1902 had called Chesnutt "the very first writer of our race" and in 1961 still averred that he "is the greatest [literary] artist we have produced."[39] However, his 1925 assessment that "Mr. Chesnutt is a storyteller of genius transformed by racial earnestness into the novelist of talent" seems more valid.[40] Even so, each of the novels had enough special appeal to be designated as Chesnutt's best. According to Helen M. Chesnutt (*Charles W. Chesnutt: Pioneer of the Color Line*), *The Marrow of Tradition*, when published, "was widely acclaimed as the most important book on the Negro question since *Uncle Tom's Cabin*. The critics . . . said that no book of the year could compare with it in dramatic power."[41] On the other hand, J. Saunders Redding has declared that "for downright power, no novel of the Negro race quite equals *The House Behind the Cedars*."[42] Meanwhile, Loggins had found *The Colonel's Dream* "the most poignantly tragic and yet perhaps the most realistic. . . ."[43] Evaluating all three novels, Sterling Brown in

1932 concurred with John Chamberlain's opinion that Chesnutt
" 'pressed on to more tragic materials and handled them as no
white novelist could have succeeded at the time in doing.' "[44]

VII   *Reevaluation*

Recognition of Chesnutt's imaginative writing outside ethnic
confines has increased steadily since World War II, and the
criticism is far less qualified. In "Social Realism in Charles W.
Chesnutt" (1953), Russell Ames finds "a remarkable quality of
Chesnutt's novels [to be] clarity and liveliness of characterization."[45] The "net effect [of "The Passing of Grandison"] is
comic in the best sense of the word," according to Richard K.
Barksdale's "Black America and the Mask of Comedy," in *The
Comic Tradition in American Literature* (1973);[46] and George E.
Kent determined that Chesnutt has not yet been equaled in his
use of "the folk's supernaturalist and conjure tradition."[47]

Edwin H. Cady includes Chesnutt among Howells's "men and
women of [the] new generation";[48] Redding holds that Chesnutt
"was a far better novelist" than the more famous Howells.[49] In
my unpublished dissertation, "Eagle with Clipped Wings: Form
and Feeling in the Fiction of Charles W. Chesnutt," I document
Chesnutt's literary competence by selective comparisons of his
writings with those of James Lane Allen, Virginia F. Boyle,
George W. Cable, Kate Chopin, Winston Churchill, Stephen
Crane, Thomas Dixon, Paul Laurence Dunbar, Harry Stillwell
Edwards, Ellen Glasgow, Joel Chandler Harris, William Dean
Howells, Thomas Nelson Page, Francis Hopkinson Smith, Ruth
McEnery Stuart, Albion W. Tourgée, and Mark Twain. On the
basis of the literary criteria, Chesnutt surpasses most of these
writers.[50]

Chesnutt's perceptive depiction of the North Carolina scene
prompted Richard Walser to include "The Bouquet" in *North
Carolina in the Short Story* (1948) and Claude M. Simpson to
choose "The Conjurer's Revenge" as one of the selections in *The
Local Colorists: American Short Stories 1857–1900* (1960).

VIII   *Literary Impact*

Chesnutt received the Spingarn Medal in 1928. In 1929 he was
still said to be "in the history of American letters the most impor-

tant writer Cleveland has ever housed."[51] Chesnutt rather than Dunbar was recognized by Margaret Just Butcher in *The Negro in American Culture* and by Hugh M. Gloster in *Negro Voices* both as "the literary Negro of his generation" and "an important trailblazer in American Negro fiction."[52]

The indebtedness of many other authors to Chesnutt is striking. James Weldon Johnson obviously looked to *The House Behind the Cedars* for his treatment of miscegenation in *The Autobiography of an Ex-Colored Man;* so did Walter White to *The Marrow of Tradition* for his handling of lynching and mob violence in *Rope and Faggott.* Environmental oppression which erupts into violence as suffered by Ben Davis in "A Web of Circumstance," Josh Green in *The Marrow of Tradition,* and Bud Johnson in *The Colonel's Dream* anticipates similar experiences by Bigger Thomas in Wright's *Native Son* and Lutie Johnson in Ann Petry's *The Street.* Chesnutt's preoccupation with genteel middle-class colored people is reflected in the treatment of such characters by both Jessie Fauset and Nella Larsen. The emotional and psychological throes of Rena Walden and George Tryon in *The House Behind the Cedars* as well as those of Tom Taylor in "The Doll" are essentially duplicated by characters of Ralph Ellison and James Baldwin. Chesnutt's sympathetic and appreciative concern for the lowly, relieved by healthy humor, is reflected in Langston Hughes's attitude toward such characters, as in the Simple stories. Two of Chesnutt's most formidable weapons, satire and irony, are also wielded effectively by writers as different as George Schuyler, Ellison, William Melvin Kelly, Ishmael Reed, and John A. Williams. Chesnutt utilized his family and other black-oriented history in much the same manner employed subsequently by Margaret Walker in *Jubilee,* Ernest Gaines in *The Autobiography of Miss Jane Pittman,* and Alex Haley in *Roots.* Like Chesnutt, both Ellison and Baldwin have notably pursued their literary ends in essays as well as in fiction. Finally, there is a growing consensus about the extent of Chesnutt's influence on the writers of the Harlem Renaissance.

IX   *Literary Contributions*

Charles W. Chesnutt's literary contributions are many. Foremost is his portrayal of the Afro-American in an unprecedented variety of authentic characterizations. His objectivity in portrayal of character, regardless of ethnicity, is noteworthy, as is also his frank, forceful treatment of themes inspired by the realities of American life. Moreover, Chesnutt's dependability in recording, relating, assessing, and sometimes interpreting produced social history of especial importance for a tempestuous period of American development.

Also of great significance are expositions in which Chesnutt strips away the façades behind which human nature too often masqueraded in nineteenth-century American literature. His aim here was not to demean, but to work for the concurrent development of human beings and the advancement of society in accordance with traditional democratic principles.

Although Chesnutt's contribution to American literature had not been appreciated sufficiently when he ended his writing career, he had received unprecedented recognition as an Afro-American author. Chesnutt was the most outstanding of the early Cleveland authors and is recognized as the first short-story writer of national note in North Carolina. He also pioneered in using North Carolina black folk life and folklore as thematic material in his writings. He was superb in his rendition of the local black dialect. Chesnutt was likewise the first Afro-American author to write with an awareness of the techniques of imaginative prose forms and the first of his race whose work was accepted for publication on an unqualified basis. "The Goophered Grapevine" was the first prose composition by a black to appear in the pages of the *Atlantic*, the most prestigious American literary magazine of the time. And Chesnutt began the contributions to literature by a "voluntary Negro" about other people on the color line.

He was the first Afro-American to produce an aesthetically satisfying novel of black life and the first to depict in such narratives a balanced and objectively treated array of both black and white characters. Chesnutt's three novels represent the first strong and artistically rendered social studies from the Afro-American point of view. *The House Behind the Cedars* affords the first authentic study of "passing." *The Marrow of Tradition* "was the first novel in American literature to depict the collision between the whites and the educated, cultivated colored people of the South,"[53] and *The Colonel's Dream* the first to utilize "the specialized [dependent] conditions of the Negro in an all-white environment."[54]

Besides the qualities already ascribed to it, Chesnutt's writing as a whole is marked by complexity and control too consistent to be attributed to chance. Aware of the indifference and hostility of his prospective readers from the outset, he sheathed his earnestness and militancy more or less in subtleties of humor, satire and irony, allusion and paradox. At the same time, however, Chesnutt sought to offset resulting ambiguities by meticulous attention to diction, rhythm, and timing. These are aspects of his conscious artistry which greatly enriched his writing but have received least attention.

Despite these accomplishments, acceptance of Chesnutt as an important author and serious consideration of him in white literary scholarship have been tardy; no significant manifestation was apparent until the late 1960s. But given today's more enlightened social attitudes, Chesnutt will inevitably gain more of the literary recognition which he deserves.

CHAPTER 9

Conclusion

No man is free who is not as free as any other man. By that test the Negro must stand or fall; and the important thing for all of us, is not whether he shall stand or fall, but that he shall have an equal chance.[1]

CHARLES W. Chesnutt was a writer of exceptional skill who followed many significant American literary traditions. Some reflect African influence. All his imaginative prose compositions, like American literature as a whole, support what Howard Mumford Jones calls "the fundamental doctrine of American life: namely, that human beings share a common quality of humanity."[2] Most of those works also have in common with the bulk of American literature the quality of being either overtly or covertly "literature of protest rather than . . . literature of complacence."[3] Chesnutt's accomplishments have special significance because they demonstrate the dynamic quality of American democracy. Further, they denote not only the coming of age of Afro-American literature but also a meaningful expansion of national writing as a whole: "art has always taken on a special native fibre before it assumes the greater breadth," and creative expression by black citizens helps to make up that "special native fibre."[4]

Though Chesnutt seemed especially adept at writing in the various genres popular at the time he was most productive, he did not reflect the *Zeitgeist* in his social attitudes. His difference is notable in connection with the race problem; he felt that adequate solution could be found in recognition of the dignity and worth of each individual. However, while he was serving his literary apprenticeship and gaining the skill to make compelling artistic appeals for such recognition, especially for Afro-Americans, the Negro was being "firmly relegated to the lower rungs" of the social and economic ladder; it was becoming increasingly apparent that "neither equality nor aspirations for equality in any department of life were for him."[5]

In addition to expressing social views contrary to the public taste, Chesnutt bore the onus of being a black writer in the United States. Unfortunately, too, as he began to treat serious aspects of the race problem more directly, his popularity began to wane. This was almost inevitable for any writer, regardless of his ethnic ties, who was fighting for the Afro-American minority in the United States of the early 1900s. Since, as a result, Chesnutt's books were not widely read, his hopes of converting a substantial number of people to his way of thinking on the race question remained unfulfilled.

In two short years Chesnutt found out that his country was not yet ready to embrace a man of his talents and principles to the extent of purchasing enough of his imaginative works to assure him of a living as an author. Chesnutt's realistic approach when the reading public preferred to be beguiled by pleasant romances, his problack sympathies when white supremacy was in vogue, and his refusal to compromise in either respect were major causes of his failure. After "Baxter's Procrustes" in 1904 and *The Colonel's Dream* in 1905, Chesnutt turned almost completely from creative writing despite his proven ability as a literary artist.

It has been speculated that Chesnutt's almost complete silence in the world of letters for nearly thirty years, until his death in 1932, was due to his disappointment at public reception of his work and the worsening of social conditions for Negroes in the United States. Whatever the reasons, it is apparent that Chesnutt's literary career was marked by both triumph and tragedy. That he started out as a person without means, without a recognized consequential literary heritage, and without formal training as a writer affirms emphatically the potential worth of the American democratic system. On the other hand, the abortive end of his writing career, whether or not precipitated by the great disparity between words and deeds in the fulfillment of the democratic ideal for blacks, was truly an American tragedy.

The creative heights to which Chesnutt might have risen had he lived in a less hostile environment or felt less responsible for promoting the Afro-American cause will never be known. In the light of the cumulative but so far inadequate assessment of his performance, Chesnutt may be regarded at present only as a minor writer in the annals of American literature. It is likely, however, that more scholarly study of all his works will improve his reputation. Moreover, Charles Waddell Chesnutt has still another important distinction. He belongs to that eminent group of Americans who have had the broad vision and the selfless courage to urge their country toward fuller realization of its great potential as a truly democratic society.

Notes and References

Preface

1. In "The Writer in Contemporary American Society," Harvey
Swados observes that "most of the financially successful writers [of the
period mentioned] were women whose names we would not even
recognize today, and most of their readers were leisure-class women, for
whom novel-reading was a pastime to fill otherwise empty hours. . ."
(Herbert Hill, ed., *Anger and Beyond* [New York, 1966], p. 62).

Chapter One

1. Charles W. Chesnutt, Journal III, April 23, 1879, Chesnutt Collection, Fisk University Library, Nashville, Tennessee, referred to hereafter
as CC, Fisk Univ.

2. "David Dodge" [O.W. Blackwell], "The Free Negroes of North
Carolina," *Atlantic* 57 (January 1886): 29. Hugh Talmage Lefler and
Alfred Ray Newsome note in *North Carolina*, rev. ed. (1954; rpt., Chapel
Hill, 1963), pp. 397–98, that "seventy per cent of the [more than 30,463]
free Negroes in North Carolina in 1860 were mulattoes."

3. Quoted from the *Charlotte Observer* of August 3, 1900, by Mat-
thew Leary Perry, "The Negro in Fayetteville," in John A. Oates, *The
Story of Fayetteville and the Upper Cape Fear*, 2nd ed. (1950; rpt.,
Raleigh, North Carolina, 1972), p. 695.

4. John Cummings, *Negro Population in the United States*, p. 57,
quoted in John Hope Franklin, *The Free Negro in North Carolina:
1790–1860* (Chapel Hill, 1943), p. 14; referred to hereafter as *The Free
Negro*; and *Eighth Census of the United States, 1860*. Of this number 465
lived in Fayetteville, according to Franklin, *The Free Negro*, p. 18. The
1850 Census of Cumberland County includes 436 colored males and 510
colored females (free). (See Oates, p. 318.)

5. Franklin, *The Free Negro*, passim.

6. Some free Negroes who owned large plantations and operated successful business establishments did not emigrate. Matthew N. Leary, for
example, served an apprenticeship in harness making and saddling in the

wholesale firm of William Warden. He eventually bought out and enlarged the business during the early 1800s. (See Perry, in Oates, p. 698.)

7. For specifics, see John C. Hurd, *The Law of Freedom and Bondage in the United States* (Boston, 1858–62), 2: 86–89 and passim.

8. Dr. Matthew Leary Perry, a descendant of a Free Man of Color, identified three "distinct classes of people" during that period: "The free white man, enjoying and exercising all the rights and privileges of an American citizen; the free colored man, deprived of nearly all the rights and privileges of an American citizen; and the colored slave, who in legal parlance, was a mere chattel." (See Perry, in Oates, p. 696.)

9. Letter dated June 29, 1900, from Chesnutt to Emmet J. Scott; CC, Fisk Univ.

10. See "Slaves Must Not Be Taught to Read," in Hugh Talmage Lefler, ed., *North Carolina History Told by Contemporaries*, 4th ed. (1934; rpt., Chapel Hill, 1965), pp. 269–70.

11. Helen M. Chesnutt, *Charles W. Chesnutt: Pioneer of the Color Line* (Chapel Hill, 1952), pp. 2–3.

12. Ibid., p. 4. Andrew Jackson Chesnutt's father, reputedly a Euro-American of some means, is not identified by name in Helen Chesnutt's biography of her father.

13. Chesnutt, Journal I, August 13, 1875; CC, Fisk Univ.

14. Journal II, 1879; CC, Fisk Univ.

15. Spingarn Medal Acceptance Speech, Los Angeles, California, July 3, 1928. This award, established by Joel E. Spingarn in 1913, is made annually to the black who has made an outstanding achievement in his field. Charles W. Chesnutt was cited for his "pioneer work as a literary artist depicting the life and struggles of Americans of Negro descent, and for his long and useful career as scholar, worker, and freeman of one of America's greatest cities." (See CC, Fisk Univ., and Helen M. Chesnutt, "Charles W. Chesnutt," *Ohio Authors and Their Books: Biographical Data and Selective Bibliographies for Ohio Authors, Native and Resident, 1796–1950*, ed. William Coyle [Cleveland, 1962], p. 115.)

16. Journal I, August 13, 1875; CC, Fisk Univ.

17. Journal I, July 16, 1875; CC, Fisk Univ.

18. Journal III, May 8, 1880; CC, Fisk Univ.

19. Journal III, April 23, 1879; CC, Fisk Univ.

20. Journal III, April 23, 1879; CC, Fisk Univ.

21. "The Rambler," *Book Buyer* 18 (June 1899): 361.

22. Journal I, August 13, 1875; CC, Fisk Univ.

23. Journal IV, March 26, 1881; CC, Fisk Univ.

24. Journal III, March 16, 1880; CC, Fisk Univ.

25. Journal II, p. 1, 1877, and Journal III, March 17, 1880; CC, Fisk Univ.

26. Journal III, May 29, 1880; CC, Fisk Univ.

27. Journal III, May 29, 1880; CC, Fisk Univ.

28. For a discussion of the agreement resulting from the disputed outcome of the presidential election of 1876, see Rayford W. Logan, *The Betrayal of the Negro from Rutherford B. Hayes to Woodrow Wilson* (New York, 1965), pp. 23–31.

29. For practice Chesnutt wrote his class lecture notes in shorthand. He also took down sermons and speeches, including one delivered by Frederick Douglass on October 1, 1880, in Raleigh, North Carolina, and "worried Susie into a positive dislike for me (reading so much)" by awakening her early in the morning and keeping her up late at night dictating to him. (See Journal III, p. 126; CC, Fisk Univ.)

Chapter Two

1. Charles W. Chesnutt, Journal III, January 30, 1881; CC, Fisk Univ.

2. Journal I, June 7, 1875; CC, Fisk Univ.

3. Journal I, July 31, 1875; CC, Fisk Univ.

4. Journal III, May 8, 1880; CC, Fisk Univ.

5. Journal III, March 30, 1880; CC, Fisk Univ.

6. Journal IV, January 21, 1881; CC, Fisk Univ.

7. Sylvia Lyons Render, July 18, 1966, interview with R. C. W. Perry, a native of Fayetteville and a nephew of Chesnutt's wife.

8. Journal II, October 16, 1878; CC, Fisk Univ.

9. Helen M. Chesnutt, p. 37.

Chapter Three

1. Charles W. Chesnutt, Journal IV, March 26, 1881; CC, Fisk Univ.

2. Journal IV, March 17, 1881; CC, Fisk Univ.

3. Letter from Chesnutt to Houghton Mifflin, September 8, 1891; CC, Fisk Univ.

4. CC, Fisk Univ.

5. See, for example, W. H. Page's letter of October 2, 1897, to Chesnutt, excerpted as follows: "It has given me great pleasure to read the two stories you sent after your return home. . . . I do not hesitate to say that I should keep one of them, most likely both, but for the reason that we have had such hard luck in making room for your other two stories which I value highly, I do not feel like keeping these when we may not be able to use them for so long a time. This field that you are working is a very profitable one I think, but we cannot give it undue attention, and I fear that the two stories that we now have are as many as we ought to commit ourselves to for the present." (CC, Fisk Univ.)

6. Sylvia Lyons Render, September 14, 1961, interview with Helen M. Chesnutt, who said that the story was inspired by an occurrence in a firm in Cleveland where her father was once employed.

7. Hugh M. Gloster, *Negro Voices in American Fiction* (Chapel Hill, 1948), p. 34.

8. Letter dated September 8, 1891, from Chesnutt to Houghton Mifflin; CC, Fisk Univ. See also letter dated February 17, 1899, from Houghton Mifflin to Chesnutt, CC, Fisk Univ.; Carolyn Shipman, "The Author of 'The Conjure Woman,' Charles W. Chesnutt," *Critic* 35 (July 1899): 632–34; and "Book Reviews: Recent Fiction," *Critic* 5 (July 1899): 650.

9. See Charles W. Chesnutt, "Post-Bellum—Pre-Harlem," *Breaking into Print*, ed. Elmer Adler (New York, 1937), pp. 53–54.

10. CC, Fisk Univ.

11. CC, Fisk Univ.

12. See, for example, the symposium, "Shall the Negro Be Educated?" (Nashville: The Open Letter Club, 1889); CC, Fisk Univ. See also "The Open Letter Club," in Arlin Turner's *George W. Cable: A Biography* (Durham, 1956), pp. 263–72, and "Open Letters," in Philip Butcher's *George W. Cable: The Northampton Years* (New York, 1959), pp. 92–107, for detailed discussions of the Open Letter Club.

13. See the letter dated April 13, 1889, from Cable to Chesnutt and Chesnutt's reply of May 3, 1889; CC, Fisk Univ.

14. See the letter of November 23, 1893, from Tourgée to Chesnutt and the latter's reply, November 27, 1893; CC, Fisk Univ. Chesnutt's assessment that public response would be slight was correct; lack of stock subscriptions forced Tourgée to abandon the project within the next six months.

15. On June 5, 1890, Chesnutt wrote Cable that he had just dined with a cultured gentleman who intimated "that he considered a mulatto an insult to nature, a kind of monster that he looked upon with infinite distaste; that a black Negro he looked upon with some respect, but any laws which permitted the intermarriage of the two races, or tended in any way to bring the two races nearer together were pernicious. . . . I fear there is too much of the same sentiment for mulattoes to make good magazine characters, and I notice that all of the many Negroes (excepting your own) in the magazine press recently, have been blacks, full blooded, and their chief virtues have been their dog-like fidelity to their old master. . . . Such characters exist. . . . But I can't. . . or rather I won't write about them." (CC, Fisk Univ.)

16. Page, formerly editor of the *Forum*, was an editor for the *Atlantic* from 1895 to 1900. He replaced Cable as Chesnutt's chief literary adviser. In addition to editorial competence and an active liberalism on race matters, Page enriched a lasting friendship between the two men with an intimate knowledge of North Carolina, his native state and Chesnutt's favorite setting.

17. See the letter of October 2, 1897, from Page to Chesnutt; CC, Fisk Univ.

18. CC, Fisk Univ.

19. See Chesnutt's letter dated December 7, 1897, to Page; CC, Fisk Univ.

20. CC, Fisk Univ.

21. Mary Tracey Earle, in "Some New Short Stories," *Book Buyer* 18 (June 1899): 399–401, found fundamental differences between the Uncle Julius and the Uncle Remus tales. In a letter to Chesnutt dated June 13, 1899, she cited Uncle Julius's conscious use of the tales as an added manifestation of Chesnutt's artistry. (CC, Fisk Univ.)

22. *The Conjure Woman* (Boston, 1899), pp. 40–41.

23. *Frederick Douglass*, "The Beacon Biographies of Eminent Americans," ed. M. A. de Wolfe Howe (Boston, 1899), p. vii.

24. Letter from Chesnutt to Houghton Mifflin, December 12, 1899; CC, Fisk Univ.

25. They are so called because, along with other physical attributes, their complexions are fair enough for the venous blood to show through the skin of the upturned wrists.

26. See William C. Brewer, "Poor Whites and Negroes in the South Since the Civil War," *Journal of Negro History* 15 (1930): 31–32. See also Brewton Berry, *Race and Ethnic Relations* (Boston, 1958), 2nd ed., pp. 319–20; Wendell Holmes Stephenson and E. Merton Coulter, eds., *A History of the South* (Baton Rouge, 1947–51), vol. 9: *Origins of the New South*, by C. Vann Woodward, pp. 205–63, 350–60, and passim, referred to hereafter as *Origins*; Rayford W. Logan, *Betrayal*, pp. 15–104; Frenise A. Logan, *The Negro in North Carolina: 1876–1894* (Chapel Hill, 1964), pp. 75–96 and passim; Gunnar Myrdal, *An American Dilemma: The Negro Problem and Modern Democracy* (New York, 1944), rev. ed., 1962, passim; and John Hope Franklin, *From Slavery to Freedom: A History of American Negroes*, Third Edition (New York, 1969), pp. 297–343, 382–451, and passim, referred to hereafter as *From Slavery*.

27. See draft of a letter written in April 1879 to the *Christian Union*, Journal III, pp. 114–15; CC, Fisk Univ.

28. CC, Fisk Univ.

29. Woodward, *Origins*, p. 350; Lefler and Newsome, p. 522.

30. CC, Fisk Univ.

31. CC, Fisk Univ.

32. CC, Fisk Univ.

33. See, for example, Charles W. Chesnutt, "A Defamer of His Race," *Critic* XXXVIII (April 1901): 350–51; CC, Fisk Univ.

34. That Chesnutt recognized the potential danger to his artistry is evident in his "The Negro in Art," *Crisis* 33 (November 1926): 28–29; CC, Fisk Univ.

35. Letter from Charles W. Chesnutt to Houghton Mifflin, December 30, 1901; CC, Fisk Univ.

36. Letter from Charles W. Chesnutt to Walter Hines Page, June 29, 1904; CC, Fisk Univ.

37. See letter of September 17, 1903, from Francis J. Garrison to

Chesnutt, and Chesnutt's letter of September 29, 1903, to Dr. Charles F. Thwing, President, Western Reserve University; CC, Fisk Univ.

38. Thomas Nelson Page, *The Negro: The Southerner's Problem* (New York, 1904), pp. 293, 81–84. Page based many of his assumptions on statements in Thomas's *The American Negro*, which had been discredited three years before *The Negro* was published. See n. 33 above.

39. Booker T. Washington Papers, Manuscript Division, Library of Congress, Washington, D.C.; and CC, Fisk Univ.

40. This and other articles on various aspects of Negro life by Booker T. Washington, W. E. B. DuBois, Paul Laurence Dunbar, Wilford H. Smith, H. T. Kealing, and T. Thomas Fortune comprise *The Negro Problem: A Series of Articles by Representative American Negroes of Today* (New York, 1903).

41. Ibid., p. 92.

42. Helen M. Chesnutt, p. 213.

Chapter Four

1. Charles W. Chesnutt, "Negro Authors," an unpublished speech delivered to members of the Colored Men's Association in Cleveland in 1918; CC, Fisk Univ.

2. *The House Behind the Cedars* (New York, 1900; rpt., Toronto, Ontario, 1969), pp. 5,6. That such a murder took place is confirmed in a letter dated July 17, 1916, from E. J. Lilly to Chesnutt, and the reply dated October 16, 1916, CC, Fisk Univ.; and Oates, pp. 220–24. See also Blackwell P. Robinson, ed., *The North Carolina Guide* (Chapel Hill, 1955), p. 199, to confirm Chesnutt's accurate description of the building.

3. Oates, p. 129, and Sylvia Lyons Render, July 18, 1966, interview with R. C. W. Perry.

4. *The House Behind the Cedars*, pp. 30–31. See also Joseph Seawell Jones, *Memorials of North Carolina* (New York, 1838), p. 74.

5. *The House Behind the Cedars*, p. 30. See also Robinson, p. 196.

6. "The Goophered Grapevine," *The Conjure Woman*, pp. 2, 3–4. Lefler and Newsome, pp. 375, 476, confirm turpentine and textiles as major industries in Cumberland County during the 1870s.

7. *The Colonel's Dream* (New York, 1905), pp. 15–16.

8. *The House Behind the Cedars*, p. 257.

9. "Uncle Wellington's Wives," *The Wife of His Youth and Other Stories of the Color Line* (New York, 1900; rpt., Ann Arbor Paperback, 1969), p. 233.

10. Ibid., p. 236.

11. In his essay "The Free Colored People of North Carolina," Chesnutt identified the Croatans as "mixed Indians and Negroes" who were recognized in the late nineteenth century by the North Carolina Legislature as having descended from a Croatan Indian tribe and the

whites of the lost colony of Virginia; see *Southern Workman* 31 (March 1902): 139.

12. See *The Conjure Woman*, p. 75.

13. Letter from Chesnutt to Walter Hines Page, May 20, 1898; CC, Fisk Univ.

14. Charles William Foster, "The Representation of Negro Dialect in Charles W. Chesnutt's *The Conjure Woman*," *Dissertation Abstracts* 29 (April 1969): 3597-A.

15. "The Goophered Grapevine," *The Conjure Woman*, p. 11.

16. "Po' Sandy," *The Conjure Woman*, p. 44.

17. *The Marrow of Tradition* (1901; rpt., New York, 1969), p. 284.

18. *The House Behind the Cedars*, p. 256.

19. "Tom's Warm Welcome," in Sylvia Lyons Render, ed., *The Short Fiction of Charles W. Chesnutt* (Washington, D.C., 1974), p. 187; referred to hereafter as *Short Fiction*.

20. "Uncle Wellington's Wives," *The Wife of His Youth*, pp. 237–38.

21. Lefler and Newsome, p. 395.

22. "Superstitions and Folk-Lore of the South," *Modern Culture* 13 (May 1901): 231.

23. Letter from Charles W. Chesnutt to Walter Hines Page, editor of the *Atlantic*, April 4, 1898; CC, Fisk Univ.

24. "Superstitions and Folk-Lore of the South," *Modern Culture* 13 (May 1901): 232.

Chapter Five

1. Charles W. Chesnutt, Journal III, March 25, 1880; CC, Fisk Univ.

2. CC, Fisk Univ.

3. Spingarn Medal Acceptance Speech, Los Angeles, July 3, 1928; CC, Fisk Univ.

4. See, for example, the "racial creed of the Southern people" proclaimed in 1913 by Thomas Pearce Bailey, a southern educator, quoted in Woodward, *Origins*, pp. 355–56.

5. Chesnutt, "Post-Bellum—Pre-Harlem," p. 56.

6. Letter from Charles W. Chesnutt to Houghton Mifflin, August 23, 1899; CC, Fisk Univ.

7. Edwin Mims, "Thomas Nelson Page," *Atlantic* 100 (July 1907): 114.

8. See above, Chapter 3.

9. W. D. Howells, "A Psychological Counter-Current in Recent Fiction," *North American Review* 173 (December 1901): 882–83.

10. Letter to Chesnutt from John S. Durham, May 9, 1899; CC, Fisk Univ.

11. In a letter of September 8, 1891, to Houghton Mifflin, Chesnutt wrote in part, "These people have never been treated from a closely sympathetic standpoint; they have not had their day in court. Their friends

have written of them, and their enemies; but this is, as far as I know, the first instance where a writer with any of their own blood has attempted a literary portrayal of them. If these stories have any merit, I think it is more owing to this new point of view than to any other thing" (CC, Fisk Univ.). Chesnutt's point is well taken, but apparently he had not then read the fiction of William Wells Brown, Frank J. Webb (whose ethnic identity is not clear), Martin Delany, Frances E. W. Harper, J. McHenry Jones, and Pauline E. Hopkins.

12. *The Conjure Woman*, pp. 108–109.

13. "Dave's Neckliss," *Short Fiction*, p. 133.

14. *The Conjure Woman*, p. 136.

15. Ibid., p. 75.

16. Ibid., p. 67.

17. *Short Fiction*, p. 131.

18. *The Conjure Woman*, p. 71.

19. *Short Fiction*, p. 107.

20. Ibid., p. 118.

21. It is still different, according to John Shelton Reed's *The Enduring South: Subcultural Persistence in Mass Society* (Chapel Hill, 1974), pp. 45 and passim.

22. Two rabbits with long upstanding ears flank the bust of a more venerable Uncle Julius on the cover of the first edition of *The Conjure Woman*. Uncle Julius is also a version of John, the archetypical Negro slave of Negro folklore who always outwits and outtalks his master. Jack in "A Matter of Principle" has both the name and the qualities of a latter-day John.

23. For amplification, see Orlando Patterson, *The Sociology of Slavery* (Rutherford, New Jersey, 1967), pp. 174–81.

24. *The Conjure Woman*, p. 88.

25. "The Passing of Grandison," *The Wife of His Youth*, pp. 178–79.

26. *The Marrow of Tradition*, p. 90.

27. Ibid., pp. 284, 309. In a letter of December 11, 1901, to Chesnutt, Charles W. Anderson expresses a typical reader reaction: "I know many Dr. Millers throughout the Southland, but you will forgive me, I know, for confessing hearty admiration for that fellow who rode on the railroad trucks, and who dies, rifle in hand, before the burning hospital. He is certainly one of the many types of which we are in need, as a race. We will never amount to a great deal until we produce a few martyrs, and in my judgement we can spare a good many . . . ministers to advantage. . . ." (CC, Fisk Univ.)

28. See the letter dated June 5, 1890, in CC, Fisk Univ.: "Judge Tourgée's cultivated white Negroes are always bewailing their fate and cursing the drop of black blood which 'taints'—I hate the word, it implies corruption—their otherwise pure race. An English writer would not hesitate to call a spade a spade, to say that race prejudice was mean and

narrow and unChristian. He would not be obliged to kill off his characters or immerse them in convents, as Tourgée does his latest heroine, to save them from a fate worse than death, i.e., the confession of inferiority by reason of color."

29. For example, even when "passing," Toinette in Tourgée's *A Royal Gentleman* is unable, when challenged, to rid herself completely of the mental attitudes and automatic responses of a slave. Moreover, in Howells's *An Imperative Duty* Rhoda Aldgate displays a "child's gaiety and lightness" and an "elfish whimsicality and thoughtless superficiality" stereotypic of Negroes before she is aware of her racial background; indeed, her primitivistic tendencies are especially attractive to Dr. Olney. (See Howells's *An Imperative Duty* [New York, 1892], pp. 66, 133. See also Anne Ward Amacher, "The Genteel Primitivist and the Semi-Tragic Octoroon," *New England Quarterly* 29 [June 1956]:216–27.)

30. Joseph Boskin, "Sambo: The National Jester in the Popular Culture," *The Great Fear: Race in the Mind of America*, ed. Gary B. Nash and Richard Weiss (New York, 1970), p. 165.

31. Henry Clay Lukens, "American Literary Comedians," quoted in Wade H. Hall, *The Smiling Phoenix: Southern Humor from 1865 to 1914* (Gainesville, Florida, 1965), p. 217.

Chapter Six

1. Charles W. Chesnutt, from an address, "Age of Problems," delivered at a meeting of the Cleveland Council of Sociology in 1906; CC, Fisk Univ.

2. See Leslie H. Fishel, Jr., "The North and the Negro, 1865–1900: A Study in Race Discrimination," unpublished Ph.D. dissertation, Harvard University, 1955; Frank U. Quillin, *The Color Line in Ohio*, University of Michigan Historical Studies (Ann Arbor, Michigan, 1913); and Myrdal, *Dilemma*, passim.

3. CC, Fisk Univ.

4. See Chesnutt's "Race Prejudice: Its Causes and Its Cure," *Alexander's Magazine* 1 (July 1905): 21.

5. CC, Fisk Univ.

6. CC, Fisk Univ.

7. [The Race Problem], address delivered to the Medina (Ohio) Coterie [1913]; CC, Fisk Univ.

8. CC, Fisk Univ.

9. CC, Fisk Univ.

10. See "Crossing the Color Line"; CC, Fisk Univ.

11. CC, Fisk Univ. Chesnutt's most caustic reaction to a white person's views on this subject is contained in his letter of November 7, 1909, to the Rt. Rev. William Brown, Bishop of Arkansas, acknowledging receipt of an autographed copy of his book, *The Crucial Race Question*. "I do not

know whether it ever occurred to you—it certainly has to me—that if the Creator had intended to prevent the inter-mixture of races, he might in His infinite wisdom have accomplished this purpose by a very simple method, as he has by the physiological laws which prevent the confusion of genera in the lower animals." (See CC, Fisk Univ.)

12. *The House Behind the Cedars*, p. 142.

13. "The Future American: A Complete Race Amalgamation Likely to Occur," *Boston Evening Transcript*, September 1, 1900, p. 24.

14. CC, Fisk Univ.

15. Mrs. Carteret and Mrs. Polly Ochiltree in *The Marrow of Tradition* are also among the white characters whose antipathy to mixed marriages coarsens their moral fiber; see pp. 254–67 and passim.

16. *The Wife of His Youth*, pp. 94, 96.

17. Ibid., p. 117.

18. Page 25. The essay had been previously delivered as an address before the Boston Literary and Historical Society on June 25, 1905.

19. "Race Prejudice," pp. 25–26.

20. CC, Fisk Univ.

21. [The Negro's Rights]; CC, Fisk Univ.

22. See "An Inside View of the Negro Question"; CC, Fisk Univ.

23. "Social Discrimination," a talk given by Chesnutt as presiding officer at a session of the first Amenia Conference. The conference was called by Joel Spingarn at Troutbeck (his estate) in Amenia, Dutchess County, New York, in August 1916, to persuade former followers of the late Booker T. Washington and other uncommitted Negro leaders to give the NAACP more support. The contents of Chesnutt's "The Status of the Negro in the United States," a paper read at the Conference of Social Workers, Cleveland, July 1912, and "The Negro in Cleveland," *Clevelander* 5 (November 1930): 3–4, 24, 26–27, indicate that these goals were still unmet even in Cleveland. His conclusion was that Afro-Americans "still have a long and hard road to travel to reach that democratic equality upon the theory of which our government and our social system are founded, not to seek which would make them unworthy [even] of contempt" (27).

24. "An Inside View of the Negro Question."

25. Charles W. Chesnutt, letter to Booker T. Washington, June 27, 1903; CC, Fisk Univ.

26. CC, Fisk Univ.

27. "Women's Rights," in "Votes for Women: A Symposium by Leading Thinkers of Colored America," *Crisis* 10 (August 1915): 182.

28. See Chesnutt letters to Washington dated June 27, 1903; August 11, 1903; March 5, 1904; November 3, 1906; March 23, 1907; November 22, 1907; October 19, 1908; and November 25, 1908; CC, Fisk Univ. See the following essays by Chesnutt: "On the Future of His People," *Saturday Evening Post* 172 (January 10, 1900): 646; "A Plea for the American

Negro," *Critic* 36 (February 1900): 160–63 (both reviews of Washington's *The Future of the American Negro*); and "The Negro's Franchise," *Boston Evening Transcript*, May 11, 1901, p. 18, in response to the address of "Dr. Donald of Trinity Church, delivered at the dedication of Dorothy Hall, Tuskegee Institute."

29. Washington letters to Chesnutt, October 29, 1906, and May 16, 1903; CC, Fisk Univ.

30. For another treatment of this issue see "The Right to Jury Service," n.d.; CC, Fisk Univ.

31. *The Marrow of Tradition*, p. 239.

32. Chesnutt declared that "the Supreme Court of the United States is in my opinion a dangerous place for a colored man to seek justice. He may go there with maimed rights; he is apt to come away with none at all." (See letter of March 22, 1899, to W. H. Page; CC, Fisk Univ.) Chesnutt criticized the Court at greater length in "Disfranchisement," *The Negro Problem*, pp. 114–16, and provided support for his stand in his analysis of far-reaching decisions of the Court on Negro rights in "The Courts and the Negro," n.d. He likewise chided the federal government and the North for permitting widespread disfranchisement in the South in "Liberty and the Franchise," n.d. (CC, Fisk Univ.).

33. Chesnutt's depiction of the deliberately cruel treatment of the prisoners is horrifying, as when Bud Johnson is goaded into fighting and escaping, only to be flogged later in attempts to break his spirit; see *The Colonel's Dream*, pp. 59–61, 210–11, 218–19.

34. Charles W. Chesnutt, "Peonage, or the New Slavery," *Voice of the Negro* 1 (September 1904): 394, 395, 396. Chesnutt also corresponded with important figures on this matter. In a letter dated May 13, 1905, Attorney General W. H. Moody sent Chesnutt a requested copy of his "Oral Argument Before the Supreme Court in the case of Clyatt v. United States" (commonly called the "Peonage Case") and related legal documents which Chesnutt may have consulted before completing *The Colonel's Dream*. See also Chesnutt's letter of June 27, 1903, to Booker T. Washington; CC, Fisk Univ.

35. CC, Fisk Univ.; and *Clevelander* 5 (November 1930): 3–4, 24, 26–27.

36. CC, Fisk Univ.; and Records of 70th Congress, First Session, 1928, Senate Committee on the Judiciary on Limiting Scope of Injunction in Labor Disputes, Pt. 4, pp. 603–609.

37. "The Status of the Negro in the United States," paper read before the Conference of Social Workers, Cleveland, Ohio, July 1912; CC, Fisk Univ.

38. "Social Discrimination," address delivered at the Amenia Conference, August 1916; CC, Fisk Univ.

39. [The Race Problem], address delivered to the Medina (Ohio) Coterie [1913]; CC, Fisk Univ.

40. See Chesnutt, "Distribution of Southern School Funds," Cable Collection/Tulane University, New Orleans, Louisiana; and the Medina Speech [1913]; CC, Fisk Univ.

41. Letter to W. H. Page, August 15, 1899; CC, Fisk Univ.

42. [The Negro's Rights]; CC, Fisk Univ.

43. CC, Fisk Univ.

44. CC, Fisk Univ.

45. See, for example, the symposium, "Shall the Negro Be Educated or Suppressed?" *Independent* 41 (February 21, 1889): 225–27.

46. "Liberty and the Franchise"; CC, Fisk Univ.

47. Chesnutt Collection, Western Reserve Historical Society; referred to hereafter as CC, WRHS.

48. For a more detailed discussion, see Chesnutt's "A Plea for the American Negro," *Critic* 36 (February 1900): 160–61, and "On the Future of his People," *Saturday Evening Post* 172 (January 10, 1900): 646. See also his "A Visit to Tuskegee," *Cleveland Leader*, March 31, 1901, p. 19.

49. C. Vann Woodward, *The Strange Career of Jim Crow*, 3rd rev. ed. (New York, 1974), pp. 35–43; referred to hereafter as *Jim Crow*.

50. Ibid., pp. 72–73.

51. CC, Fisk Univ.

52. CC, Fisk Univ.

53. Quoted in Woodward, *Jim Crow*, pp. 49–50.

54. See "The Courts and the Negro" and "Social Discrimination"; CC, Fisk Univ.

55. See Chapter 4, n. 2.

56. Sylvia Lyons Render, interviews with Mrs. E. T. Page and Mrs. Irene Cherry in Nashville, Tennessee, on December 28, 1961; and with Mrs. Fannie Headen in Chicago, Illinois, on February 18, 1962.

57. Thomas Nelson Page, "The Lynching of Negroes—Its Cause and Its Prevention," *North Carolina Review* 178 (January 1904): 3–48.

58. *Historical Statistics of the United States: Colonial Times to 1957* (Washington, D. C., 1960), p. 218. See also Chesnutt's Medina Speech [1913]; CC, Fisk Univ.

59. Condensed from Franklin, *From Slavery*, pp. 439–44; R. W. Logan, pp. 347–52; Myrdal, pp. 558–69; and William M. Tuttle, Jr., *Race Riot: Chicago in the Red Summer of 1919* (New York, 1970), pp. 3–31.

60. It is perhaps more than coincidental that one of the members of the "Committee of Colored Citizens" who replied to the "Declaration of White Independence" demanding the expulsion of editor Manley and the dismantling of his press was also named Josh Green.

61. *Independent*, p. 5. See also Medina Speech [1913]; CC, Fisk Univ.

62. North Carolina Congressman George H. White, the last Afro-American to serve in Congress after 1901 until 1929, introduced the first such bill in 1900. Neither this proposed piece of legislation nor more than

ten others introduced in Congress through 1937 cleared both the House and the Senate despite continued effort by the NAACP and citizens like Chesnutt, who also made substantial annual contributions to the pioneer civil rights organization.

63. "An Inside View of the Negro Question," 1889; CC, Fisk Univ.

64. Roland C. McConnell, "The Negro in North Carolina Since Reconstruction," Ph.D. dissertation, New York University, 1945, p. 210.

65. Letter of September 7, 1888, from Attorney John S. Leary to Chesnutt and one of October 2, 1888, from A. H. Slocumb to Chesnutt; CC, Fisk Univ.

66. Josephus Daniels, *Editor in Politics*, quoted in Helen G. Edmonds, *The Negro and Fusion Politics in North Carolina: 1894–1901* (Chapel Hill, 1951), p. 154. See also McConnell, p. 210; William Alexander Mabry, *The Negro in North Carolina Politics Since Reconstruction* (Durham, North Carolina, 1940), pp. 44–56; and Lefler and Newsome, pp. 520–22.

67. CC, Fisk Univ.

68. N.d.; CC, Fisk Univ.

69. See Chesnutt's letter of May 27, 1904, to Robert C. Ogden. For his efforts to get before the public news which most white papers would not print, see letter of September 6, 1913, from Charles T. Halliman to Chesnutt about an article by Jessie Fauset (later well known as a novelist) critical of the "segregation situation in Washington"; Chesnutt's reply of September 15, 1913; and an initial letter of September 24, 1913, to Miss Fauset. All in CC, Fisk Univ.

70. CC, Fisk Univ.

71. W. E. Burghardt DuBois, *The Souls of Black Folk: Essays and Sketches* (Chicago, 1903; rpt., New York, 1970), p. 17; and Chapter 2, n. 3, above.

72. *The A.M.E. Church Review*, October 1913, p. 103.

73. CC, Fisk Univ.

74. "A Solution for the Race Problem," speech [1915]; CC, Fisk Univ.

75. [The Race Problem], address before the Ohio State Night School, February 1928; CC, Fisk Univ.

76. "A Solution for the Race Problem," speech [1915]; CC, Fisk Univ.

77. CC, Fisk Univ.

Chapter Seven

1. Charles W. Chesnutt, "The Relation of Literature to Life," address before the Bethel Literary and Historical Association, Washington, D.C., October 7, 1913; CC, Fisk Univ.

2. Chesnutt explains in "The Negro in Present Day Fiction," n.d., that no Afro-American literary tradition was viable when he began writing; CC, Fisk Univ.

3. CC, Fisk Univ.

4. CC, Fisk Univ.

5. CC, Fisk Univ.

6. Journal V; CC, Fisk Univ.

7. CC, Fisk Univ.

8. Letter of Chesnutt to W. H. Page, June 29, 1904; CC, Fisk Univ.

9. *Short Fiction*, p. 158.

10. "The Writing of a Novel," n.d.; CC, Fisk Univ.

11. *The House Behind the Cedars*, p. 227. See also p. 239 of the novel for Plato's inflated opinion of Tryon.

12. Booker T. Washington Papers, Manuscript Division, Library of Congress, Washington, D.C.

13. "The Writing of a Novel," n.d.; CC, Fisk Univ.

14. "The Writing of a Novel," n.d.; CC, Fisk Univ.

15. CC, Fisk Univ.

16. See *The Conjure Woman*, pp. 199, 203; and *The House Behind The Cedars*, p. 257.

17. "The Goophered Grapevine," *The Conjure Woman*, p. 4. For a similar treatment, see *The Colonel's Dream*, pp. 15–16. See also pp. 1, 9–10 of *The Marrow of Tradition* for another illustration of this technique.

18. CC, Fisk Univ.

19. Journal III, March 16, 1880; CC, Fisk Univ.

20. *The Colonel's Dream*, p. 112.

21. Speech [Niagara Movement, Oberlin], 1908; CC, Fisk Univ.

Chapter Eight

1. Charles W. Chesnutt, quoted in a letter dated June 19, 1928, to Chesnutt from Harry G. Smith, "Editor and Owner," *Cleveland Gazette*; CC, Fisk Univ.

2. Quoted in Chesnutt's letter of March 25, 1902, to Horace Traubel, ed., "The Conservator"; Traubel Papers, Manuscript Division, Library of Congress, Washington, D. C.

3. N.p., n.d.; CC, Fisk Univ.

4. Letter of May 9, 1899, to Chesnutt; CC, Fisk Univ.

5. See Henderson letter of June 10, 1899, to Chesnutt, CC, Fisk Univ.; and *Book Buyer* 18 (June 1899): 399–401. See also Earle letter of June 13, 1899, to Chesnutt; CC, Fisk Univ.

6. Florence A. H. Morgan, "Novel Notes," *Bookman* 9 (June 1899): 373.

7. Anon., "Book Reviews: Recent Fiction," *Critic* 35 (July 1899): 650.

8. Page 421.

9. See W. D. Howells, "Mr. Charles W. Chesnutt's Stories," *Atlantic* 85 (May 1900): 700–701.

10. Carolyn Shipman, "The Author of 'The Conjure Woman,' Charles W. Chesnutt," *Critic* 35 (July 1899): 634.

11. Horace Traubel, *"The Wife of His Youth," Conservator* 12 (February 1902): 188, and *"The Conjure Woman," Conservator* 13 (November 1902): 139.

12. Traubel Papers, Library of Congress, Washington, D. C. Marked copies of all Chesnutt's books of fiction, some with clippings of reviews, more correspondence, and other notations, are also among the papers.

13. Anon., "Review of *The House Behind the Cedars,*" *Lakeside Magazine*, May 1901, p. 53; Anon., "Review of *The House Behind the Cedars,*" *Nation* 72 (February 21, 1901): 182; and Anon., "A Negro's Book," *Pittsburgh Post*, December 2, 1900; quoted in Curtis W. Ellison and E. W. Metcalf, Jr., comp., *Charles W. Chesnutt: A Reference Guide* (Boston, Mass., 1977), pp. 44, 43, 37, respectively.

14. N.d., n.p., clippings; CC, Fisk Univ.

15. N.d., n.p., clippings; CC, Fisk Univ.

16. According to Helen M. Chesnutt (p. 178), this novel "was an acknowledged literary success—it had been accepted by the Booklovers Library and was classed by the *Outlook* among the twenty-five books of literature of the year [1901]. . . . " This is especially significant for a period during which "the romantic glow persisted, even among those critics whose eyes should have been opened by this time . . . most Americans [also] persisted in taking an unrealistic survey of themselves and their era." (Quoted from Grant C. Knight, *The Critical Period in American Literature* [Chapel Hill, 1951], p. 147.)

17. Letter from Barnett to Chesnutt, November 5, 1901; CC, Fisk Univ.

18. CC, Fisk Univ.

19. CC, Fisk Univ.

20. Letter from Garrison to Chesnutt, November 9, 1901; CC, Fisk Univ.

21. Clipping; CC, Fisk Univ.

22. 54: 582. See also Chesnutt's letter of March 20, 1902, to publisher George H. Mifflin, in which the apology offered privately to the latter by the publisher of the *Independent* is discussed; CC, Fisk Univ.

23. For a more explicit condemnation, see the *Wilmington Messenger* for January 7, 1902:

Chesnutt has already written a lying account of what happened at Fayetteville, North Carolina, in which he maligned whites and gratified his own ego. Now Chesnutt has written a book of lies and slander that is teeming with fabrications and bitterness. Despite the fact that we have not seen the book, we have seen it reviewed and so know the truth of it. Chesnutt is particularly slanderous in the way he misrepresents the riot that took place in Wilmington [Wellington]. In that case the blacks themselves brought it on.

24. W. D. Howells, "A Psychological Counter-Current in Recent Fiction," *North American Review* 173 (December 1901): 882–83. In a letter of November 10, 1901, to Henry B. Fuller, Howells called Chesnutt "an artist almost of the first quality; as yet too literary, but promising things hereafter that will scarcely be equalled in our fiction." Howells's awareness of the racial strictures which Chesnutt condemns in *The Marrow of Tradition* probably prompted him to continue: "Good Lord! How such a Negro must hate us." See Mildred Howells, ed., *Life in Letters of William Dean Howells* (New York, 1968) 2: 149.

25. Chesnutt's letter of December 30, 1901, to Houghton Mifflin; CC, Fisk Univ.

26. *The National Cyclopaedia of American Biography* 12: 266, s.v. "Charles Waddell Chesnutt."

27. Letter of June 24, 1904, from Page to Chesnutt; CC, Fisk Univ.

28. Letter of September 18, 1905, from Chesnutt to Ward; CC, Fisk Univ.

29. Letter to Chesnutt, September 20, 1905; CC, Fisk Univ.

30. Letter dated October 14, 1905; CC, Fisk Univ.

31. See letter from Lilly to Chesnutt, July 9, 1916; CC, Fisk Univ.

32. See, for example, reviews in the *Buffalo Express*, December 10, 1899; *Chicago Chronicle*, December 25, 1899; *Minneapolis Times*, January 7, 1900; *New York Times Book Review*, January 13, 1900; *San Francisco News*, January 27, 1900; and *Current Literature*, June 1900. The *Minneapolis Times* notes, "What Mr. Washington is doing for the material and social side of the Negro's progress, Mr. Chesnutt is doing for the spiritual side." See Ellison and Metcalf, pp. 18, 22, 24, 26, 30.

33. See "A Forcible Writer," *Cleveland Gazette*, July 9, 1899, and the *Washington* (D.C.) *Times*, October 5, 1900; cited in Ellison and Metcalf, pp. 15, 31.

34. Page 411.

35. Herman Dreer, ed., *American Literature by Negro Authors* (New York, 1950), p. 229, and William Garson Rose, *Cleveland: The Making of a City*, p. 613.

36. Alain Locke, "The Negro in American Literature," *New World Writing*, ed. Arabel J. Porter (New York, 1952), p. 27.

37. Vernon Loggins, *The Negro Author: His Development in America to 1900* (New York, 1934, rpt., Port Washington, N.Y., 1964), pp. 316, 324.

38. Ibid., p. 312. See also Benjamin Brawley's favorable assessment of Chesnutt's writing in "The Negro in American Literature," *Bookman* 56 (October 1922): 137–41, which Chesnutt himself found "a *very* fine critical estimate of my writings." Statement made in a letter of July 7, 1924, to Miss L. M. Barnett (CC, WRHS).

39. Braithwaite letter of November 29, 1902, to Chesnutt (CC, Fisk Univ.), and statement by Braithwaite to Sylvia Lyons Render in New York City on November 17, 1961.

40. William Stanley Braithwaite, "The Negro in American Literature," *The New Negro*, ed. Alain Locke, p. 43.

41. Page 176.

42. See *To Make a Poet Black*, p. 73. For a similar opinion, see also Carl Milton Hughes, *The Negro Novelist: A Discussion of the Writings of American Negro Novelists 1940–1950* (New York, 1953), p. 42.

43. Loggins, p. 328.

44. "In Memoriam: Charles W. Chesnutt," *Opportunity: Journal of Negro Life* 10 (December 1932): 387. For a similar appraisal see Ernest Kaiser, "Literature on the South," *Freedomways* 4 (Winter 1964): 149–67.

45. *Phylon* 14 (1953): 206.

46. *The Comic Tradition in American Literature*, ed. Louis D. Rubin, Jr. (New Brunswick, N.J., 1973), p. 352.

47. George E. Kent, "Patterns of the Harlem Renaissance," in *The Harlem Renaissance Remembered*, ed. Arna Bontemps (New York, 1972), p. 29.

48. *The Realist at War: The Mature Years 1885–1920 of William Dean Howells* (Syracuse, 1958), p. 208.

49. J. Saunders Redding, "The Problems of the Negro Writer," *Massachusetts Review* 6 (Autumn-Winter 1964): 61.

50. George Peabody College for Teachers, 1962, passim. For a later ranking of Chesnutt with three major figures in this group, see Robert Bone, *Down Home: A History of Afro-American Short Fiction from Its Beginnings to the End of the Harlem Renaissance* (New York, 1975), p. 105.

51. Elrick B. Davis, "Reading and Writing," *Cleveland Press*, February 2, 1929, p. 3.

52. Butcher, *The Negro in American Culture* (New York, 1957), p. 278; Gloster, p. 46.

53. Helen M. Chesnutt, p. 176.

54. Loggins, cited by Carl Milton Hughes, p. 42.

Chapter Nine

1. Charles W. Chesnutt, letter of September 17, 1908, to William E. Walling; CC, Fisk Univ.

2. Howard Mumford Jones, *Ideas in America* (Cambridge, 1944), p. 201.

3. Ibid.

4. Van Wyck Brooks, "Preface," in Constance Rourke, *The Roots of American Culture*, ed. Van Wyck Brooks (New York, 1942), p. vi.

5. Woodward, *Jim Crow*, pp. 6–7.

Selected Bibliography

PRIMARY SOURCES

All unpublished material is in the Chesnutt Collection at Fisk University except where noted.

1. Novels, Published

The Colonel's Dream. New York: Doubleday, Page & Company, 1905.
The Conjure Woman. Boston: Houghton Mifflin Company, 1899.
The House Behind the Cedars. New York: Houghton Mifflin Company, 1900.
The Marrow of Tradition. Boston: Houghton Mifflin Company, 1901.
The Wife of His Youth and Other Stories of the Color Line. Boston and New York: Houghton Mifflin Company, 1899.

2. Novels, Unpublished

A Business Career. [ca. 1898].
Evelyn's Husband. [ca. 1900].
Mandy Oxendine. [ca. 1897].
Paul Marchand, F.M.C. (Free Man of Color). [ca. 1928].
The Quarry. [ca. 1928].
The Rainbow Chasers. [ca. 1900].
Rena. N.d., various versions. Revised and published as *The House Behind the Cedars*.

3. Biography

Frederick Douglass. In *The Beacon Biographies of Eminent Americans Series*, ed. M. A. de Wolfe Howe. Boston: Small, Maynard and Co., 1899.

4. Drama

"Mrs. Darcy's Daughter." A play in 4 acts. [ca. 1906].

174

5. Short Fiction, Published

"Appreciation," *Puck* XXI (April 20, 1887): 128.
"Aunt Lucy's Search," *Family Fiction*, April 16, 1887; clipping.
"Aunt Mimy's Son," *Youth's Companion*, March 1, 1900; clipping.
"The Averted Strike," *The Short Fiction of Charles W. Chesnutt*, ed.,
    Sylvia Lyons Render. Washington, D.C.: Howard University Press,
    1974, pp. 383–90. Referred to hereafter as *Short Fiction*.
"Baxter's Procrustes," *Atlantic* 93 (June 1904): 823–30.
"The Bouquet," *Atlantic* 64 (November 1899): 648–54.
"Busy Day in a Lawyer's Office," *Tid Bits*, January 15, 1887; clipping.
"Cartwright's Mistake," *Cleveland News and Herald*, September 19,
    1886.
"Cicely's Dream," *The Wife of His Youth and Other Stories of the Color
    Line*. Boston and New York: Houghton Mifflin Company, 1899,
    pp. 132–67. Referred to hereafter as *The Wife of His Youth*.
"Concerning Father," *Crisis* 37 (May 1930): 153–55, 175.
"The Conjurer's Revenge," *Overland Monthly* 13 (June 1889): 623–29.
"Dave's Neckliss," *Atlantic* 64 (October 1899): 500–508.
"A Deep Sleeper," *Two Tales*, March 11, 1893, pp. 1–8; clipping.
"The Doll," *Crisis* 3 (April 1912): 248–52.
"The Dumb Witness," *Short Fiction*, pp. 153–63.
"The Goophered Grapevine," *Atlantic* 60 (August 1887): 254–60.
"Gratitude," *Puck*, December 1888; clipping.
"The Gray Wolf's Ha'nt," *The Conjure Woman*, pp. 162–94.
"Her Virginia Mammy," *The Wife of His Youth*, pp. 25–29.
"Hot-Foot Hannibal," *Atlantic* 83 (January 1899): 49–56.
"How Dasdy Came Through," *Family Fiction*, February 12, 1887, pp.
    21–22.
"Jim's Romance," *Short Fiction*, pp. 343–52.
"The Kiss," *Short Fiction*, pp. 306–14.
"A Limb of Satan," *Short Fiction*, pp. 195–201.
"Lonesome Ben," *Southern Workman* 29 (March 1900): 137–45.
"The March of Progress," *Century* 61 (January 1901): 422–28.
"The Marked Tree," *Crisis* 29 (December 1924): 59–64, and 29 (January
    1925): 110–13.
"Mars Jeems's Nightmare," *The Conjure Woman*, pp. 64–102.
"A Matter of Principle," *The Wife of His Youth*, pp. 94–131.
"McDugald's Mule," *Family Fiction*, January 15, 1887; clipping.
"A Miscarriage of Justice," *Short Fiction*, pp. 357–64.
"The Origin of the Hatchet Story," *Puck* 25 (April 24, 1889): 132.
"An Original Sentiment," n.p., n.d., clipping.
"The Partners," *Southern Workman* 30 (May 1901): 271–78.
"The Passing of Grandison," *The Wife of His Youth*, pp. 168–202.
"Po' Sandy," *Atlantic* 61 (May 1888): 605–11.

"A Secret Ally," [New Haven, Conn.] *Register*, December 6, 1887; clipping.

"The Sheriff's Children," *Independent*, November 7, 1889, pp. 30–32.

"Sis Becky's Pickaninny," *The Conjure Woman*, pp. 132–61.

"Stryker's Waterloo," *Short Fiction*, pp. 365–73.

"The Sway-Backed House," *Outlook* 66 (November 1900): 588–93.

"Mr. Taylor's Funeral," *Crisis* 9 (April 1915): 313–16, and 10 (May 1915): 34–37.

"A Tight Boot," *Cleveland News and Herald*, January 30, 1886; clipping.

"Tobe's Tribulations," *Southern Workman* 29 (November 1900): 656–64.

"Tom's Warm Welcome," *Family Fiction*, November 27, 1886; clipping.

"Uncle Peter's House," *Cleveland News and Herald*, December 1885; clipping.

"Uncle Wellington's Wives," *The Wife of His Youth*, pp. 203–68.

"A Victim of Heredity," *Short Fiction*, pp. 123–31.

"The Web of Circumstance," *The Wife of His Youth*, pp. 291–323.

"White Weeds," *Short Fiction*, pp. 391–404.

"The Wife of His Youth," *Atlantic* 82 (July 1898): 55–61.

"Wine and Water," *Family Fiction*, April 23, 1887; clipping.

6. Short Fiction, Unpublished

"The Hand of God." N.d., Chesnutt Collection, Western Reserve Historical Society, Cleveland, Ohio. Referred to hereafter as CC, WRHS.

[Mr. Peyton and Miss Wrenn.] [ca. 1897].

7. Essays, Poems, and Speeches—Published

"Abraham Lincoln: An Appreciation," *Southwestern Christian Advocate* 43 (February 4, 1909): 1, 8.

"Advice to Young Men" (under pseudonym Uncle Solomon), *Social Circle Journal* 18 (November 1886): n.p.

"A Battle Hymn" (poem), *Social Circle Journal* 18 (October 1886): n.p.

"A Defamer of His Race." *Critic* 38 (April 1901): 350–51.

"The Disfranchisement of the Negro," *The Negro Problem: A Series of Articles by Representative American Negroes of Today*. New York: James Pott & Company, 1903, pp. 79–124.

"The Free Colored People of North Carolina," *Southern Workman* 31 (March 1902): 136–41.

"The Future American; A Complete Race Amalgamation Likely to Occur," *Boston Evening Transcript*, September 1, 1900, p. 24.

"The Future American; A Stream of Dark Blood in the Veins of Southern Whites," *Boston Evening Transcript*, August 25, 1900, p. 15.

"The Future American; What the Race Is Likely to Become in the Process of Time," *Boston Evening Transcript*, August 18, 1900, p. 20.

"Lincoln's Courtship," *Southwestern Christian Advocate* 43 (February 4, 1909): 8.

"Methods of Teaching." Paper read at the annual meeting of the North Carolina Teachers Association, November 23, 1882, and included in the printed proceedings, pp. 5–13.

"The Mission of the Drama," *Cygnet* 1 (January 1920): 11–12.

"A Multitude of Counselors," *Independent* 43 (April 2, 1891): 4–5.

"The Negro in Art," *Crisis* 33 (November 1926): 28–29.

"The Negro in Cleveland," *Clevelander* 5 (November 1930): 3–4.

"The Negro's Franchise," *Boston Evening Transcript*, May 11, 1901, p. 18.

"Obliterating the Color Line," [Cleveland] *World*, October 23, 1907; clipping.

"On the Future of His People," *Saturday Evening Post* 172 (January 10, 1900): 646.

"Peonage, or the New Slavery," *Voice of the Negro* 1 (September 1904): 394–97.

"A Plea for the American Negro," *Critic* 36 (February 1900): 160–61.

"Post-Bellum—Pre-Harlem," in *Breaking into Print*, ed. Elmer Adler. New York: Simon and Shuster, 1937, pp. 47–56.

"Race Ideals and Examples," *A.M.E. Church Review* 30 (October 1913): 101–17. Adapted from Address, "Ideals and Their Realization," delivered at Wilberforce University, June 12, 1913.

"Race Prejudice; Its Causes and Its Cure," *Alexander's Magazine* 1 (July 1905): 21–26. Address delivered before the Boston Literary and Historical Association, June 25, 1905.

"Superstitions and Folk-Lore of the South," *Modern Culture* 13 (May 1901): 231–35.

"Things to Be Thankful For" (under pseudonym Uncle Solomon), *Social Circle Journal* 18 (October 1886): n.p.

"A Visit to Tuskegee," *Cleveland Leader*, March 31, 1901; clipping.

"What Is a White Man?" *Independent* 4 (May 30, 1889): 5–6.

"Women's Rights," in "Votes for Women: A Symposium by Leading Thinkers of Colored America," *Crisis* 10 (August 1915): 182–83.

8. Essays, Poems, and Speeches—Unpublished

"Abraham Lincoln," February 14, 1928.

"The Advantages of a Well Conducted Literary Society," October 1881. A lecture delivered before the Normal Literary Society, Fayetteville, N.C.

"Age of Problems." Address before the Cleveland Council of Sociology in 1906.

"Alexander Dumas," n.d. Address before the Rowfant Club, April 11, 1914.

"The Courts and the Negro," n.d.

"Crossing the Color Line," n.d.

Diary, 1896; CC, WRHS.

"Etiquette; Good Manners," 1881. Lecture to the Normal Literary Society, Fayetteville, N.C.

"George Meredith." Address to the Rowfant Club, May 11, 1916.

[The Ideal Nurse.] Address at Provident Hospital and Training School, Chicago, Ill., May 4, 1914.

"An Inside View of the Negro Question." 1889.

[Introduction to Reading from an Unpublished Story.] Speech to the Electrical League of Cleveland, December 28, 1916.

"Joseph C. Price, Orator and Educator: An Appreciation," n.d.; CC, WRHS.

Journals and Notebooks, July 1, 1874–September 13, 1885.

"Liberty and the Franchise," n.d.

[Literary Outlook of Colored Men in Literature.] n.d.

[Meeting of Colored Citizens.] May 31, 1892.

[The Negro in the American Revolution.] Address delivered on the occasion of the Perry Centennial, Cleveland, Ohio, September 14, 1913.

[Negro Authors.] Address before the Colored Men's Association, Cleveland, Ohio, ca. 1918.

"The Negro in Books." Address delivered during the "Buy a Book Movement" in Philadelphia, December 1916.

"The Negro in Latin America," [ca. 1913].

"The Negro in Present Day Fiction," n.d. Address delivered at the Dunbar Forum, Oberlin, Ohio.

[The Negro Question.] January 1926.

"The Negro's Franchise; a Right He Must Struggle to Maintain," n.d.

[The Negro's Rights.] Address before the Bethel Literary and Historical Association, Washington, D.C., October 19, 1908.

[Niagara Movement: Oberlin.] October 1908.

[The Race Problem.] Address to the Medina Coterie, Medina, Ohio, [March 25, 1913].

[The Race Problem.] Address at the Ohio State High School, Cleveland, Ohio, February 1928.

"The Relation of Literature to Life." Address before the Bethel Literary and Historical Association, Washington, D.C., October 7, 1913.

[Report on Negro Migration and Its Effects.] n.d.; CC, WRHS.

"The Right to Jury Service," n.d. (after May 1910).

"Self-Made Men." Lecture to the Normal Literary Society, Fayetteville, N.C., March 10, 1882.

"Social Discrimination." Address at the Amenia Conference, August 1916.

"A Solution for the Race Problem," n.d.

[Speech to Business Men.] [ca. 1930].

[Spingarn Medal Acceptance Speech.] Los Angeles, July 3, 1928.

"The Status of the Negro in the United States." Paper read before the Conference of Social Workers, July 1912.

[St. Francis of Assisi.] n.d.

[The Term Negro.] n.d.

"To the Public," 1920.

[Valentines I.] n.d.; CC, WRHS.

[Valentines II.] n.d.; CC, WRHS.

"Who and Why Was Samuel Johnson?" Address delivered before the Rowfant Club, November 11, 1911.

"Why Do We Live?" n.d.

[Why I Am a Republican.] n.d.

[World War I.] n.d. Address before the colored soldiers at Cleveland Armory, n.d.

"The Writing of a Novel," n.d.

SECONDARY SOURCES

African Folklore. Ed. Richard M. Dorson. Garden City, N.Y.: Doubleday, 1972. Detailed discussion of the significance of African folklore to the folklorist.

African Myths and Tales. Ed. Susan Feldman. New York: Dell, 1963. Introduction treats the origin, nature, and functions of African folktales, of which examples are also provided in categories.

BRAITHWAITE, WILLIAM STANLEY. "The Negro in American Literature." *The New Negro.* Ed. Alain Locke. New York: Albert and Charles Boni, 1925. A short but balanced appraisal of Chesnutt as a literary artist by a perceptive Afro-American poet/critic.

BRAWLEY, BENJAMIN GRIFFITH. *The Negro in Literature and Art in the United States.* New York: Dodd, Mead, 1934; rpt. St. Claire Shores, Michigan: Scholarly Press, 1972. A succinct assessment of Chesnutt's literary acumen by a noted black scholar.

BRITT, DAVID D. "Chesnutt's Conjure Tales: What You See Is What You Get." *CLA Journal* 15 (1972): 269–83. An astute literary analysis and interpretation of the Uncle Julius tales in *The Conjure Woman.*

Charles W. Chesnutt: A Reference Guide. Comp. Curtis W. Ellison and E. W. Metcalf, Jr. Boston: G. K. Hall, 1978. A substantial chronological listing of Chesnutt criticism which reflects the range of reaction to his writings.

CONRAD, EARL. *The Invention of the Negro.* New York: Paul S. Eriksson, 1966. A tracing of the cultivation of antiblack sentiment in the United States for several hundred years.

DAVIS, RUSSELL H. *Black Americans in Cleveland: From George Peake to Carl B. Stokes 1796–1969.* Washington, D.C.: Associated Publishers, 1972. A well-researched account of Negro life in Cleveland, including some firsthand observations of Chesnutt's personal and professional life.

DORSON, RICHARD M. *American Folklore.* Chicago and London: University of Chicago Press, 1959. An extensive treatment of Afro-American folklore.

FRANKLIN, JOHN HOPE. *From Slavery to Freedom.* 3rd ed. New York: Alfred A. Knopf, 1967. A reliable account of Chesnutt's time from a black perspective.

GAYLE, ADDISON, JR. *The Way of the New World: The Black Novel in America.* Garden City, N.Y.: Anchor Press/Doubleday, 1976. A provocative, ideologically oriented discussion of Chesnutt's novels.

GLICKSBERG, CHARLES L. "The Alienation of Negro Literature." *Phylon* 11 (1950): 49–58. An insightful probing of the psychological impact upon Chesnutt of writing under marked negrophobic conditions.

GLOSTER, HUGH M. *Negro Voices in American Fiction.* Chapel Hill: University of North Carolina Press, 1948. A comparative evaluation of Chesnutt as fiction writer in an account of the historical development of Afro-American literature.

HIGGINBOTHAM, A. LEON, JR. *In the Matter of Color/Race and the American Legal Process: The Colonial Period.* New York: Oxford University Press, 1978. A scholarly study which confirms Chesnutt's repeated charge that the formulation and administration of laws were racist.

HOVET, THEODORE R. "Chesnutt's 'The Goophered Grapevine' as Social Criticism." *Negro American Literature Forum* 7 (1973): 83–85. A convincing argument that social protest may enhance the literary quality of even a folktale.

JOINT COMMITTEE OF THE NORTH CAROLINA ENGLISH TEACHERS ASSOCIATION AND THE NORTH CAROLINA LIBRARY ASSOCIATION. *North Carolina Authors: A Selective Handbook.* Chapel Hill: University of North Carolina Press, 1952. A ranking of Chesnutt among North Carolina writers.

KELLER, FRANCES RICHARDSON. *The American Crusade: The Life of Charles W. Chesnutt.* Provo, Utah: Brigham Young University Press, 1978. A largely chronological account of Chesnutt's life and writings. Based on documentation and speculation, this work purports to trace Chesnutt's ancestry.

LOGGINS, VERNON. *The Negro Author: His Development in America.* New York: Dodd, Mead, 1934; rpt. Port Washington, N.Y.: Kennikat

Press, 1964. A white scholar's detailed evaluation of Chesnutt as a writer of fiction within a historical context.

McMahan, Margaret. "A Tar Heel Literary Pioneer." *Fayetteville Observer*, November 11, 1962, Sec. D., pp.1–2. An assessment of Chesnutt as the first writer to put Fayetteville on the literary map of the United States.

Modern Language Association, American Literature Group. *Report of the Committee on Trends in Research in American Literature, 1940–1950.* Baton Rouge, Louisiana: Modern Language Association, 1951. A report which reflects the increase of scholarly interest in Chesnutt as an imaginative writer.

Nolen, Claude H. *The Negro's Image in the South: The Anatomy of White Supremacy.* Lexington: University of Kentucky Press, 1967. An exposition on the entrenched doctrine of white supremacy articulated at the end of the nineteenth century which impelled Chesnutt to protest.

Oden, Gloria C. "Chesnutt's Conjure as African Survival." *Melus*, Spring 1978, pp. 38–48. Praise of Chesnutt's use of black folk beliefs and customs.

Parker, John W. "Chesnutt as a Southern Town Remembers Him." *Crisis* 56 (July 1949): 205–206; 221. Recollections of Chesnutt as a youth and young adult in Fayetteville by local residents.

Redding, J. Saunders. *To Make a Poet Black.* Chapel Hill: University of North Carolina Press, 1939; rpt. Great Neck, N.Y.: Core Collections Books, 1978. A discussion of Chesnutt's artistry and the impact of a hostile literary environment upon it.

Turner, Arlin. "Dim Pages in Literary History: The South Since the Civil War." *Southern Literary Study: Problems and Possibilities.* Ed. Louis D. Rubin, Jr., and C. Hugh Holman. Chapel Hill: University of North Carolina Press, 1975. A perceptive essay supporting Chesnutt's stance on protest.

Walcott, Ronald. "Chesnutt's 'The Sheriff's Children' as Parable." *American Negro Literature Forum* 7 (1973): 86–88. A refutation of the argument that protest reduces the literary quality of a story.

Woodward, C. Vann. *Reunion and Reaction.* Boston: Little, Brown, 1951. A white revisionist's account of the trends and events of the latter part of the nineteenth century which perturbed Chesnutt.

Index